From Fame to Captain Forbes and the loss of the *Schomberg*

Shannon Azzaro

Front cover: a painting of the "Schomberg Aground" by Philip J. Gray, courtesy of the artist.

Back cover: "New School: Sixty Days to Australia" [Schomberg] 1855. Print of lithograph, Berlin, Druck u. Verlag v. F. Silber. Courtesy of the National Library of Australia

Cover design by Cathy Larsen

First Published 2022
Copyright © 2022 Shannon Azzaro

National Library of Australia Cataloguing-in-Publication entry:
Creator: Azzaro, Shannon, author.
Title: From Fame to Infamy: Captain Forbes and the loss of the Schomberg
ISBN: 978-0645486001
Subjects: Shipwrecks: Forbes, James Nicol, 1821-1874: Schomberg (Ship)

Tale Publishing
Melbourne Victoria

Tale

Contents

Author's Note

Acknowledgements and Postscript

Diaries and Letters

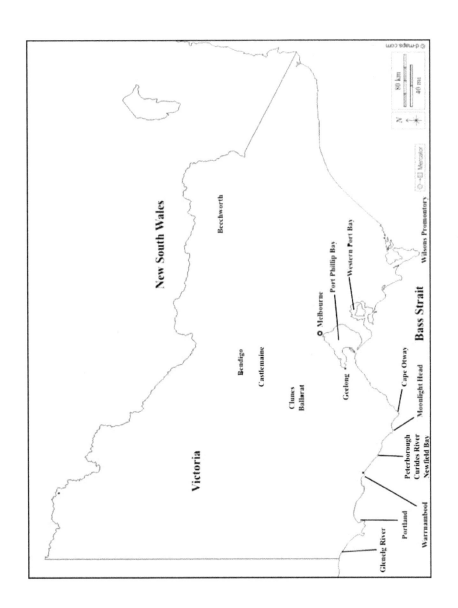

Places in Victoria mentioned in the text.
Courtesy of D-Maps https://d-maps.con/carte.

Author's Note

Historians, sailors, and shipwreck enthusiasts have published many versions of the shocking tale of Master Mariner, Captain "Bully" Forbes, who wrecked the mighty clipper *Schomberg* along the Victorian Shipwreck Coast[1] in 1855. Why write another account when others must have well-covered the sources of information?

Some years ago, I wondered if any previously undiscovered information about the shipwreck could be found in historic newspapers, Australian and British, now readable online. I began to read and almost at once had serious reservations about the incredible stories that circulated and were reported in the newspapers, resulting in public outrage.

I first read sources from the time of the disaster. These included newspapers, three *Schomberg* shipboard diaries and those of a dozen different passengers in other sailing ships of the day. Then I considered a number of general maritime histories. Almost without exception, writers published their narratives 50 to 150 years after Forbes' death. These all were informative, important writings, but

---

[1] Shipwreck Coast stretches from Cape Otway west to Port Fairy

most authors came to the one conclusion about Captain Forbes: if a complicated man, he was essentially a villain and rightly branded forever as infamous. I set out to see where my research might lead. My impression was that writers had revealed only part of the story.

In the weeks after the catastrophe, Captain Forbes was publicly portrayed as a drunk, a gambler, a womaniser, a risk to the moral wellbeing of colonial Melbourne, a rude, violent, cruel man, disinterested in the safety of his passengers and one who might have deliberately scuttled his prized vessel. Was the journey a case of "Hell or Melbourne in 60 days?" Did Forbes bring about his own downfall? Was his reputation ruined by others, and if so, why?

There will be readers familiar with the story of "Bully" Forbes and the loss of the *Schomberg*. But here, the whole story is told in greater detail, set against the events of the day.

This work should interest the descendants of those who sailed from the British Isles to Australia in the *Schomberg* or any other ship under sail in the nineteenth century, and readers attracted to the era of the tall ships.

Shannon Azzaro

1: An Extraordinary Decade, the 1850s

This decade was a time of spectacular change for Britain and some of her colonies, old and new. A series of significant events coincided in these years, stimulating shipbuilding, international trade, travel, and great emigrations. In Britain, merchants valued shipping companies that ran fast vessels with adventurous captains who strove for short voyages to distant ports. One particular captain in Liverpool had gained fame as a skilled navigator and daring mariner, outstanding in the practice of his craft: Captain James Nicol Forbes. His record-breaking return voyage from Liverpool to Melbourne in 1852 as Captain of the *Marco Polo* was well-known. Three years later, in 1855, at the launch of the new British ship *Schomberg*, one guest speaker referred to Forbes as the "fastest man of the age," at a time when both passengers and merchants desired quicker travel to even the farthest destinations.

Like many other European countries such as France, Spain, Italy, and the Netherlands, Britain practiced mercantilist economic policy from the 16th to the early 19th century. There was government regulation of the economies, each protecting its wealth and power at the expense of rival nations. British legislation prevented other countries from trading with her colonies and required colonial products to be exported only to Britain. Raw materials were produced in the colonies and shipped back to Britain's manufacturers. The finished goods were then exported to the colonies for sale in their markets. Such legislation protected emerging British industry and maintained the shipbuilding industry within the realm. Britain relied on her merchant shipping fleet to supplement her Navy during times of conflict. The British Navy commissioned the merchant shipping fleet during the 1850s as troop and equipment carriers for the Crimean War, 1853-56, and the Indian Mutiny of 1857.

~

In the 1840s British merchants and captains of industry were increasingly in favour of moving away from protectionism towards free trade. Manufacturing required additional raw materials from other countries. Men like Sir Robert Peel campaigned to cease the application of import tariffs on foreign-grown grains to make simple food affordable for the poorest people. Parliament repealed the *Navigation Acts* in 1849. Britain and her colonies then engaged freely with others and opened their trade to most foreign nations. Subsequently, the sailing ships that entered British ports were a sight to behold. America had acquired independence from Britain and could experiment without the constraints of British shipbuilding regulations and had moved far ahead of the British shipping industry. Ships now visiting British ports included the *Witch of the Wave*, the *Sovereign of the Seas*, and even the much smaller stylish racing yacht *America*. These impressed shipbuilders and seafarers in the United Kingdom. Britain had few big ships at that time: not many were registered at more than 500 tons capacity.[2] While there had been continual advances in shipbuilding in Britain, around 1850 there was quite a gap between the sleek and fast ships in the American fleet and ships in British ports. Britain needed to add similarly fast ships to her merchant fleet if she was to compete with rival nations.

~

In the British Isles, increasing population was becoming a problem. There was such population growth in the first half of the nineteenth century that in just 50 years, the numbers had doubled. There was a great surge in emigration to Britain's present and former colonies during the decade, including to antipodean Australia. At the same time, Australians were calling for more self-funded immigrants and an end to convict transportation. Population growth in the Australian colonies had been continuous but slow and steady. Then came a staggering increase in migrant numbers arriving on Australian shores. They came principally from the British Isles but also small numbers from other countries.

Gold was the big game-changer. Once discoveries of gold fields were announced, in New South Wales in 1851 and in 1852 more extensive goldfields in Victoria, migration to these two colonies increased massively. Australian settlers wrote letters home describing the riches diggers gathered from the earth. On his return from Melbourne to Liverpool in the *Marco Polo*, British newspapers reported Captain Forbes saying that his recent passengers had easily found employment in Melbourne. Younger single ladies were "set for life," and even those

---

[2] MACGREGOR, David R. *Fast Sailing Ships: their design and construction, 1775-1875*. Second, revised edition. London, Conway Maritime Press Ltd.,1988. p.129

women no longer youthful were of interest to the excess of single men. The *Marco Polo*, on its first voyage to Melbourne in 1852, was the largest vessel to arrive in Port Phillip. When she anchored, small boats surrounded her, and men in the boats apparently threw small nuggets of gold amongst the passengers.[3] Gold fever also struck those already living in Australia. Colonial workers of all kinds abandoned their posts and went to the diggings. As a consequence, there was a shortage of labour. Immigrants came from England, Ireland, Scotland, Wales, and to a lesser extent, from Europe and North America. Prices and wages in Melbourne rocketed. Edwin Bird, a passenger in the *Marco Polo* 1853, described tent settlements along Melbourne's beaches in his diary.[4] There was insufficient affordable accommodation.

~

In this decade, most of those who arrived in Port Phillip remained as settlers. Some may have intended to return to the British Isles but never did. Some lucky people found a gold fortune and went home to England as very wealthy men. Others acquired local property or started businesses and found wealth that way. In England, some feared that ordinary colonials, even freed convicts, might return well-heeled to the mother country and upset traditional class arrangements.

~

Gold along the creeks and rivers soon became harder to find, and those men who had arrived without skills to offer the colonies found themselves unemployable unless they settled for less. In one diary, the writer described his shock at seeing his gentleman friend from England having to wash

---

[3] "Later from Australia" *Morning Post* (London) 28 Dec 1852 p.6
[4] BIRD, Edwin Diary of Edwin Bird. Marco Polo 1853.

his own dishes.

Before the Australian gold discoveries, most emigrants leaving the British Isles chose America and Canada as their destinations, as they were closer to home and the fares were cheaper. Britain and Europe had experienced unrest, wars, revolutions, dislocation, and famines. The Irish suffered from starvation and diseases that quickly brought down the malnourished. At least a million Irish persons died between 1845 and 1847, and another two million emigrated from their homes over the following decades. For the labouring poor of Britain, working conditions were difficult. The work could be physically damaging, and there were no pensions to support a family where the head of the household lost a limb or broke his back. Families often lived in crowded, unhealthy quarters, taking work where they could find it, struggling to stay out of debt. They hoped to find a more secure living by migrating to the colonies. For most, there were opportunities. Life in the Australian cities and countryside was far from easy but improved with some luck and considerable hard work.

~

An early census of persons in the colony of Victoria did not include the 40,000 men who had come in the early 1850s from China as sojourners, temporary citizens to the goldfields, and the original people who were already living there when the British first arrived. The first populations of the Australian continent are today termed the First Nations. They lived successfully in this land for tens of thousands of years as hunter-gatherers with sophisticated belief systems, customs, languages, laws, and complex social organisation. The first white settlers in Australia were British convicts. Britain established its first colony in Australia in New South Wales. After the American War of Independence

1775-1783, American colonies were no longer available to Britain as a destination for convicts. The First Fleet, a convoy of eleven vessels from England, arrived on the east coast of Australia in 1788, carrying equipment and stores to establish the colony, and about 750 convicts and 550 sailors, soldiers, and families. After 1802 the colony of New South Wales sent convicts and soldiers to Tasmania. From 1818 the island received a steady stream of convicts, altogether 70,000 men, women, and children. Western Australia was a British penal colony between 1826 and 1868. In the 84 years, 1778-1862, the Australian colonies received 162,000 convicted criminals, almost one-fifth of those sentenced by British courts during that period.[5]

During the 1850s, 602,000 people arrived in Australian ports: 230,000 of these were assisted passengers,[6] with part or all their fare paid for them. A benevolent individual or society financially sponsored some migrants. But in large part, they were funded by land sales within the Australian colonies. The British Land and Emigration Commission was formed in 1840 to manage funds raised by selling colonial land. Its agents were to select migrants from the unemployed or underemployed poor who, as workers, would be an asset to the colonies. The Commissioners also dealt with land grants in the bounty schemes, financial incentives offered by individual colonies such as New South Wales, Tasmania, and after 1860 by Queensland. Colonial employers ideally hoped for skilled workers and families, including agricultural labourers, shepherds, carpenters, blacksmiths, masons, wheelwrights, tailors,

[5] NATIONAL GEOGRAPHIC SOCIETY *Australian Encyclopaedia* New South Wales 5th ed 1988. SHAW, A.G.L. "Convicts and Transportation" p. 811
[6] "Immigration" *Australian Encyclopaedia.* p.1608

seamstresses, female domestic and farm servants. Naturally, not all who arrived were a boon to the workforce, whether they had arrived through convict transportation or as free settlers.

~

As immigrants arrived in their thousands in this decade, there was chaos, social and economic, as populations doubled and tripled: between 1851 and 1861, the numbers grew as follows:

New South Wales	197,265 to 357,362
Tasmania	69,187 to 89,908
Victoria	97,489 to 539,764
South Australia	66,538 to 130,812
Western Australia	7,186 to 15,936

Queensland was part of NSW until 1859, but her population measured 34,367 in 1861.[7]

The census taken in Victoria in 1854 found the population's origins: 92,172 were from England; 37,199 from Ireland; 33,716 from Scotland, and 2,280 from Wales.

~

Between October 1847 and December 1851, the Land and Emigration Commission contracted 146 ships to send to New South Wales and the Port Phillip district, with 37,754 subsidised passengers. In the following five years, 380 such ships carried 131,466 assisted migrants to the two colonies.

Non-convict numbers of arrivals in the Australian colonies, 1788 to 1860, were in the following proportions:

---

[7] ABS table "Population of the Australian Colonies, 1851-1900" In CLARK, C.M.H. *Select Documents in Australian History 1851-1900* Angus and Robertson, Sydney 1955 pp.664-5

	Assisted	Unassisted	Total
NSW	157,000	79, 000	236,000
Tasmania	81,000	12,000	93,000
Victoria	98,000	236,000	334,000
South Australia	68,000	9,000	77,000
Western Australia	6,000	11,000	17,000

Victoria separated from New South Wales in 1851 and became an individual British colony. [8]

~

In 1847 Mr. James Baines of Liverpool established a small shipping business. Then in 1849 came news of Californian gold discoveries. Within three years, diggers had also found gold in the Australian colonies. The number of people wishing to migrate to Britain's Australian colonies rapidly rose. James Baines' ambitions grew, and with associates, he founded a larger shipping company, James Baines & Company of Liverpool, in 1851. This Company established a subsidiary, the Black Ball Line of clippers, to service their Australian run. The latter was crucial to the Company's decade of great success.

~

By 1850 Captain James Nicol Forbes had been working in Liverpool for several years and had gained a reputation as a talented ship's commander. James Baines had already employed Forbes by 1849. In mid-1851, Forbes completed his training for the Master's Certificate, just as British emigrant demand for the Australian passage was taking off. Captain Forbes was in the right place at the right time. In 1852 Baines nominated Forbes to take the *Marco Polo* to Melbourne for the Land and Emigration Commission with

---

[8] "Immigration" op. cit. *Australian Encyclopaedia*

960 financially-assisted migrants.[9] She didn't look like a promising ship, but her general construction enabled her to be fast. Forbes easily pushed her to success. He achieved remarkably fast sailing times, arriving in Melbourne in an astounding 68 days and returning to Liverpool in just 76. Having returned to Liverpool, he visited the Exchange, and the merchants who were present enthusiastically applauded him for his record-beating sailing times. [10] For the merchants, Forbes had shown a return voyage taking less than six months was possible, enabling two voyages per year. Forbes' star was rising.

---

[9] PROV *Unassisted Passenger List* for *Marco Polo* arrival of Sept 1852 shows 952 immigrants' names.
[10] "Arrival of Marco Polo from Australia" *Times* (London) 14 September 1853 p.7

An early photograph of the *Schomberg* in Aberdeen. No
known copyright restriction. Image courtesy of the State
Library of South Australia.

2: James Nicol "Bully" Forbes

Firstly, and importantly, there's a need to reconsider the definition of "bully." Over the last centuries, this word has carried different meanings. Dictionaries tell us the word "bully" appeared in the play *Midsummer Night's Dream*, 1600. Shakespeare refers to Bottom the weaver, the comic relief: "O sweet bully Bottom," an early term meaning sweetheart. In the novel *Tom Sawyer*, 1876, Huck Finn says: "That's bully. Plenty bully enough for me. Just you gimme the hundred dollars, and I don't need no di'monds." But a more appropriate definition is the following: keelmen and miners working the coalpits in northeast England commonly used the term. Their meaning was "brother, comrade, or companion."[11] The keelmen loaded coal on keelboats, flat-bottomed vessels, carrying large loads of coal to waiting ships in deeper water.

How was the word used in the days of sail? Many readers will be familiar with the line from a well-known sea

---

[11] https://en.wikipedia.org/wiki/Keelmen_https://wordhistories.net/2017/11/09/origin-of-bully/ accessed 29 Dec 2021

BULLY, the champion of a party, the eldest male person in a family. Now generally in use among the keelmen and pitmen to designate a brother, companion, or comrade. In Cumberland, and also in Scotland, **billy** is used to express the same idea as **bully**."

chanty, which accompanied the task of hauling the halyards, the rope and tackle that raised sails: "*Blow the man down, bullies, blow the man down.*" Here bullies could mean comrades or mates. Aboard sailing ships, sailors sang to set a pace for their work. When heavy work was called for, to set the rhythm, the sailors sang together, with a chanty-man singing the verses and the group joining in for the chorus.

A few ship captains of the day had the epithet "bully" added to their name - Bully Waterman, Bully Hayes, Bully Martin, Bully Bragg. These were fast-sailing sea captains in the days of the tall ships. At least one of them, by reputation, a truly brutal man, rumoured to have shot a man down from the ship's rigging for insubordination. Just as some words change meaning over time, times change, and people's values change. Today we should not immediately judge the thinking or behaviour of people in the 1850s, by our current expectations or standards.

Cecily Fox-Smith was an accomplished English writer and poet in the early years of the 20th century. She was well-versed in the knowledge of sailors' yarns and seaside sailor towns. She wrote that having the term bully added to your name did not necessarily mean you were a bully in the sense in which we use the word today.[12] Forbes, you might think, was bully in the notion of being a fearless, courageous leader, commanding the rugged men in his crew.

Liverpool maritime society acknowledged Forbes as a daring seaman who could make the most of any ship, make any sailing ship go faster. By the early 1850s, with notably short voyages under his belt, he had become a most

---

[12] SMITH, Cicely Fox *Sailor Town Days* London, Methuen 1923 p. 121

prestigious mariner. In March 1853, as the *Marco Polo* was about to leave Liverpool for a second trip to Melbourne with Forbes, attendees at an event hosted by his employers, paid tribute to his talents. Such events known as dejeuners were shipboard luncheons, intended to raise the profile of the Company and attract publicity, with civic leaders and merchants as guests. Captain Forbes and his First Officer, C. McDonnell, were hailed as heroes as the *Marco Polo* sat in Salthouse Dock, Liverpool. People in business at the luncheon presented some engraved silverware to Forbes praising his achievements in his last voyage, his kindness to his 960 passengers, the good management of his crew, and the record sailing times.[13]

~

Forbes was Captain in two voyages to Melbourne of the *Marco Polo* and then the *Lightning*. In the latter, he took 64 days from Liverpool to Melbourne. In comparison, the ship *Lady McNaughton* sailed in 1850 from Plymouth to Adelaide. She travelled the Admiralty route to the Cape of Good Hope and across the Indian Ocean. A smaller ship, a barque of 850 tons, with cargo and passengers, she took 138 days to make the passage. The usual time taken by sailing ships from England to Australia before 1850 was more than one hundred days, sometimes much more. The colonies had not yet made public the discovery of gold, so perhaps speed was not the captain's goal. Two years later, passengers hoped to reach the colonial goldfields quickly before the gold ran out.

A diarist tells us they passed many slower ships during the 1853 second sailing of the *Marco Polo* to Melbourne.

---

[13] "Australian Clipper Ship Marco Polo. Presentation to Capt. Forbes" *Liverpool Mercury* 1 Mar 1853, and "Race Round the World" *Argus* 1 Jun 1853 p.4

One of the vessels they caught up with was the *Halifax* from London. She had been out 116 days. Her captain was amazed to hear that the *Marco Polo* had only been out from Liverpool for 75 days. In building his fleet, Baines favoured North American ships, which were readily available, at a reasonable price, and were excellent performers. Any vessel that didn't perform well was sold.

Captain Forbes, James Nicol Forbes, was Scottish, born on November 16, 1821, and raised in Aberdeen. James Nicol, his father, was an advocate who held important positions within the city. Forbes' parents did not marry, but the Nicol family likely supported and educated James as a child, perhaps even raising him. In those days, parents paid to have their son apprenticed at sea. In 1854, in his third captaincy of a passenger vessel, the *Lightning*, Forbes took with him on the round voyage his half-sister, who had been unwell, Isabella Nicol. He referred to her as his sister, so their relationship was close. As it happened, she met Blakiston Robinson, also travelling in the First Cabin. They married in Melbourne and began life in Australia. In time, all four of Forbes' half-sisters migrated to Victoria. Isabella Jaffray Nicol first, then Louisa Penelope, Mary Anne, and Elizabeth Rose.[14]

~

As a boy, Forbes attended a special school to learn navigation skills under Mr. Milne in Marischal Street, Aberdeen. In 1833 he went to sea as an apprentice in the merchant navy. Later, in 1839, he moved from Glasgow to Liverpool. There, in 1845 James Nicol Forbes had his first appointment as Mate. Four years later he was given the

---

[14] HIRSCH, Wendie Robinson et al. *Robinson Boys and their Highfield, Nicol and Hollinworth Families.* Published by the author, 2009 pp. 142-147

command of the new ship *Wilson Kennedy* 1130 tons, delivering it from Quebec to Liverpool, then *Cleopatra* 421 tons, from Liverpool to London, and the *Maria* 1014 tons, from Liverpool to Africa. New legislation required that he gain his Master's Certificate, which he did in Liverpool in mid-1851. Then he was Captain of three emigrant ships owned by the Black Ball Line - the *Marco Polo* 1625 tons (3000 tons burthen) for two return voyages, the *Lightning* 2000 tons (3500 tons burthen), and then the *Schomberg* 2284 tons (3500 tons burthen).[15]

~

In 1849 Forbes married Scottish-born Jane Duncan in Liverpool. Their daughter Margaret Jane Nicol Forbes was baptized at St. Peter's Church in Liverpool in February 1851. The English census of that year recorded that Jane Forbes and her small baby lived in Toxteth Park, south of Liverpool central. Jane did not enjoy good health and died in September 1864 of liver and stomach disease. Captain Forbes remarried in 1866 to Mary Anne Bellman. They had a son James Nicol Forbes, who was baptized in Liverpool in 1867. In 1871 the family was living in West Derby, east of Liverpool.[16]

~

Captain Forbes usually brought with him a selection of the latest English newspapers for the press in Melbourne. Also, in 1853 he took a painting of the *Marco Polo* by the esteemed Liverpool marine artist Samuel Walters to Melbourne, which depicted the vessel in full sail, passing the Crosby Lightship. Forbes intended to present this work

---

[15] Figures listed in the newspaper *Liverpool Mercury* 17 Nov 1854 p.4 in "Advertisements". Burthen or burden: the weight a vessel might carry.
[16] "*England and Wales Census 1871*" collection title within *FamilySearch*. www.familysearch.org

to the Melbourne Town Hall.[17] Today, however, it seems to be in private hands overseas.

~

At last, the *Schomberg*: With this majestic, much anticipated, clipper ship, Forbes left Liverpool for Melbourne on October 6th, 1855, one day later than scheduled, reportedly delayed by the tide in the Mersey. Mind you, writers have stated that Sundays were Forbes' lucky days for departure. At the time, the Liverpool seafaring community held Forbes in the highest regard. A journalist for the *Liverpool Journal* wrote at length about the mighty *Schomberg* and congratulated Messrs. James Baines and Co. for appointing a gentleman such as James Nicol Forbes to command her.[18] Much was expected of Captain Forbes and this new vessel, the largest wooden vessel built in a British shipyard.

---

[17] "Departure of the Marco Polo for Australia" *Chester Chronicle*, 19 March 1853 p.2
[18] "Schomberg" *Liverpool Journal* 22 Sep 1855, reprinted *Sydney Morning Herald* 1 Jan 1856 p.4

3: The Glorious Clipper *Schomberg* and James Baines & Company

A clipper is any sailing vessel built to be fast: sleek in design, with a shaped and elongated hull, and a sharp bow to cut through the sea with reduced resistance. Shipbuilders have always experimented with design. Before 1836, measuring a ship's capacity concentrated on length and breadth and ignored depth. Officials applied taxes and port duties based on this calculation. The old measure tempted shipowners to request deep, narrow ships from builders to reduce the tonnage. A balance was needed to keep vessels seaworthy. In 1836 the authorities established a different method for calculating a ship's capacity. So new ships were wider in some parts, narrower in others, yet with a reduction in taxable tonnage. At the water line the vessels were widest for stability.[19] The gradual evolution of the clipper style saw streamlined ships with taller masts, slightly reclined, wider, heavier spars, and great volumes of sail.

Throughout history, shipping companies and shipyards have built vessels to meet particular purposes. It is not the case that all ships in the mid or later nineteenth century

---

[19] "Steam to Australia in Thirty Days" *Adelaide Observer* 30 Dec 1854, p.10

were large. There were always many small and some larger vessels: some carried passengers and little cargo; some made short trips around the coast to another port; others traversed the oceans to distant destinations. Even the extreme distance in sailing from England to Australia did not oblige shipping companies to send bigger vessels.

~

When James Baines started his merchant shipping business, he first made some money by buying one or two second-hand ships, sending them abroad, and then selling them. Four years later, he formed a partnership with Thomas Miller Mackay, and then their business excelled, buoyed massively by the coincidental discovery of gold in Australia. While the Australian run was most important to the Company, they had other ships that sailed to all other parts of the globe. In 1849, Baines acquired the *Deborah* and the *Cleopatra*, and in 1851, the first vessel purchased by the Baines-Mackay partnership was the *Maria*.

Early in the 1850s, James Nicol Forbes captained the *Cleopatra* and the *Maria*. The record sailing time in 1852 to Melbourne and back in the *Marco Polo* excited would-be emigrants and merchants alike and boosted the Company's prospects. Baines advertised this achievement in their newspaper advertisement of sailing schedules. At a later date, when announcing upcoming sailings, it was claimed the Company brought more migrants to Australian shores than any other.[20] In Liverpool there were several merchant shipping lines, as there were in other British ports. Like its competitors, Baines & Co. endeavoured to be the most successful shipping line of the day. The Australian fleet from Baines consisted of ships such as the *Marco*

---

[20] Advertisements & Notices *Liverpool Mercury* 10 Feb 1854 p.4

Polo, John and Lucy, Boomerang, Champion of the Seas, James Baines, Lightning, Ocean Chief, Oliver Lang, Saldhana, Donald McKay, Indian Queen, and the *Schomberg.* In the 1860s, the Company sent such vessels as the *Flying Cloud, Light of the Age, Fiery Star, Golden Empire, Light Brigade, Young Australia, Sunda,* and *Montmorency* to Moreton Bay, Queensland.

On the next page is an artwork depicting the American clipper *Sovereign of the Seas,* which docked in Liverpool in 1853. The image is courtesy of the State Library of Victoria from the Brodie Collection, in the La Trobe Picture Collection. This ship contrasted greatly with the typical vessels in the English fleet. A full description of this famous vessel is given in "Sovereign of the Seas" *Shipping Gazette and Sydney General Trade List* Dec 5 1853 p. 367.

According to a contemporary critic, r. James Baines, after completing an education at a "third-class school," started work as a young apprentice clerk in his uncle Richard Baines' shipbroking business in Poole Lane (now South Castle Street), Liverpool. He was employed alongside men who were described as "jolly, brisk little fellows who could almost talk a corpse back to life."[21] Baines spent his adult life involved in one or another aspect of Liverpool's shipping industry. This city was the principal English port on the west coast, three miles down the Mersey from the open sea, well-positioned to import goods like cotton and wool for the mills and export manufactured products from the counties Lancashire and West Riding in Yorkshire. In 1858, in Liverpool, there were 25 docks along 6 miles or so on the north side of the Mersey.[22]

---

[21] ORCHARD, R.G. cited in STAMMERS, Michael K. *Passage Makers.* Brighton, Sussex, Teredo Books 1978 pp. 28, 30, 53
[22] https://historic-liverpool.co.uk/old-maps-of-liverpool/hilliars-guide-to-liverpool-1858/#4/71.66/-79.00u accessed 29 Dec 2021

Sovereign of the Seas image courtesy of the State Library
of Queensland.

In February 1854, Baines advertised ten sailings to Australia in the year's remaining months: eight of the scheduled vessels were new, purchased from North America. [23] Altogether in the years 1851 to 1854, the Company purchased 32 vessels: a meteoric expansion.

According to Basil Lubbock (English historian, sailor, and prolific maritime history writer), in 1860, James Baines & Co. owned 86 ships and employed 300 officers and 3000 sailors.[24] While the Company purchased some vessels as new, it purchased many others secondhand. They leased extra ships when needed. James Baines was quite the salesman, good at drumming up business, and quick to report their successes to the papers. Some men thought he was boastful and arrogant in his quest for success. Sir William Forwood wrote that Baines could never find a hat big enough to "contain his big head." [25] Basil Lubbock described Baines in a derogatory sense, as a "little self-made man." Baines came from a family in a lower level of Britain's stratified society than these two writers. Yet maritime specialist Michael Stammers wrote that even in the most challenging times, Baines' business associates remained with him and supported him.[26] In the last days of his shipping company his associates were still the same men.

Thomas Miller Mackay was a longtime business partner of Baines', not reflected in the company name, but equally

[23] Advertisements & Notices *Liverpool Mercury* 10 Feb 1854 p.4 op. cit.
[24]LUBBOCK, Basil *Colonial Clippers* Brown, Son & Ferguson Ltd, Glasgow Reprinted 1968 p.19 and online via archive.org
[25] FORWOOD, William B., Sir *Reminiscences of a Liverpool Shipowner* Liverpool, H. Young, 1920 p. 51
and *https://archive.org/details/reminiscencesofl00forwuoft* accessed 26 Feb 2022
[26] STAMMERS, Michael K. *Passage Makers*. Brighton, Sussex, Teredo `Books Ltd. 1978

involved in the business behind the shop-front. The Company originally also had two junior partners, Joseph Greaves and John Taylor. In the boom years, the Company's business model relied on mortgages: they purchased a vessel and borrowed against this to buy another. When the banking industry stumbled, Baines' business was at risk as banks called in debts.

In 1851 an American shipping company based in New York was already using the name, the Black Ball Line. Still, curiously, it was adopted by Baines and associates for their fleet of ships on the Australian run. Michael Stammers thought this was underhand and an act of theft. Both shipping lines used the same house flag a red, swallow-tailed pennant with a black ball at the centre. Baines' flag contained a smaller black ball than the American one, but otherwise was identical.

This Aberdeen-built *Schomberg* was a marvel in British ship construction. She was massive by the day's standards, a tall, full-rigged sailing ship built between 1854-55 by the highly regarded shipbuilders Messrs. Hall of Aberdeen. Their shipyards lay at the exit of the River Dee into the North Sea in northeast Scotland. The *Schomberg* was a wooden ship with three decks, three masts, heavy wide spars, and an enormous expanse of sail. Her main mast was estimated to weigh 15 tons. The mainyard measured 111 ft 6 in which was impressively large. The shape of her hull was in the style known as the "Aberdeen bow," lengthened and run out to form a cutwater to slice through the sea.

Halls first demonstrated this bow in their schooner, *Scottish Maid*, built in 1839. She had raked masts, inclined toward the aft, a lengthened jib-boom, an overall longer deck and hull in proportion to the width at the beam and the depth of the hold, with sharpened lines on the leading edge.

Once in the water, the *Schomberg*'s entrance lines were also long and elegant. Her top deck length from stem to stern measured 262 ft; her entire length was 288 ft; the extreme breadth was 45 ft, and her depth of hold was 29 ft 9 in. The tonnage in the new measurement post-1836 was 2284 tons, and her burthen (the calculated weight of cargo she might carry) was 3500 tons. Incidentally, *Scottish Maid* was owned by Alexander Nicol, merchant, ship-owner, younger brother of Forbes' father James Nicol.[27]

~

According to Andrew Murray, writing for the *Encyclopaedia Britannica*, 8th edition 1861, in the entry for shipbuilding, her frames were of British oak, fixed at 4.5 ft intervals. Her planking consisted of four layers of Scotch larch, each one, two and a half inches thick. The builders added the planks according to an unusual principle: the first two layers were fixed in an alternating diagonal position, passing under the bottom of the inside keel. Builders added a third layer in a perpendicular alignment, like the beams. The shipwrights also fitted a layer of larch between the frames. Between each layer, there was a thickness of felt and Archangel tar. They added a longitudinal layer of pitch pine outside, over everything, averaging 6 inches thick. Workers fastened all the layers together with wooden treenails of African oak. Murray referred to the *Schomberg* as "a specimen of a first-class Aberdeen clipper."[28] He stated the less usual method of construction, sheathing with diagonal planking, used by Alexander Hall & Son, was

---

[27] HIRSCH op. cit. p. 148-151

[28] MURRAY, Andrew "Shipbuilding" *Encyclopaedia Britannica* 1861, enlarged and reprinted two years later as a booklet *Ship-Building in Iron and Wood*. Reprinted in the Classics Reprint series. Forgotten Books, 2015. Also, now online at
https://archive.org/details/shipbuildinginir00murr

"practised in the first half of the nineteenth century by Annesley, Seppings, Fletcher & Fearnall and others."

During the 1850s, it came into practice again, and the two yards which then built ships with diagonal planking and the minimum of frames were J. & R. White at Cowes on the Isle of Wight, and Halls of Aberdeen. David MacGregor, a modern British expert in the design and development of ships, gave a detailed, technical account of the construction. He named 15 vessels constructed with planking on the diagonal in the first half of the nineteenth century.[29] Hall & Sons built the much smaller clipper *Vision* with diagonal planking of less thickness than that used in the *Schomberg*. The *Vision* was wrecked in 1857 some distance inland along the Yangtse River in China.

A half model of the *Schomberg*'s hull exists in the Riverside Museum in Glasgow, but the finished ship varied in some details from the model. Halls constructed their ships from aft, moving forward: sometimes as construction progressed, there were modifications. It was not unusual for alterations to occur in the shipyard as the building of any craft proceeded. Hall & Sons were pleased with the *Schomberg* but thought she might even have been 50 feet longer. The shipbuilders' plans used in the dockyard were lost in a fire at the offices of Halls during the Second World War. Therefore, the description and drawings provided by Andrew Murray, published in 1861, are an essential source of her characteristics and dimensions.

Several Australian papers reprinted an article from a Liverpool newspaper that described the layout of the *Schomberg*, understood by the author to mean the following. Her proportions were enormous. She could carry

---

[29] MACGREGOR op. cit. pp. 140-141

18,000 yards of sail. For the First Cabin passengers, she was luxurious: their dining room was well lit, with numerous large mirrors, walls painted in gold and white, crafted woodwork in oak, mahogany, and rosewood, and fabrics of velvet, satin, and damask. In addition, there was a good library of some 400 books. The Company added pens to house dozens of live animals: such as pigs, fowls, and a milking cow. In the lowest level of the craft were the tanks containing 90,000 gallons of water.

The top deck or main or weather deck of the vessel was flat. At the stern or the rear of this deck was a poop structure housing the Captain and Officers. Steps (the word used by the journalist at the time) led to a deck on top of the poop, which was also flat to suit the passengers taking the air. At the other end of the main deck at the stem was a forecastle, leading to the accommodation of the ordinary seamen and a large area for those men to carry out bulky work. The top of the forecastle also served as a promenade for passengers, a full topgallant deck. A moveable house covered the main hatchway in the middle of the top deck. When travelling in rough seas, this helped prevent seawater washing around the deck, and racing down into the lower levels. On the stern side of this hatchway was constructed a deckhouse for "working" the ship, carrying out usual seaman's tasks. On the other side of the hatchway was a roundhouse (so-called, not round on every vessel) housing a saloon and large dining room for the First Cabin passengers. Below the main deck, there were 60 First Cabin staterooms with portholes. The Second Cabin berths were at the front of this deck under the seamen's quarters. Below all were the well-ventilated Third Cabin areas. The lowest deck areas were for storage and the hold for goods and cargo. Below all, the ship held immense water tanks.[30]

The image below is from Hathi Trust's superior scan of the illustration of the *Schomberg*'s Body Plan from Andrew Murray's entry in the *Encyclopaedia Britannica* 1861 and 1863 booklet *Ship-Building in Iron and Wood.*[31]

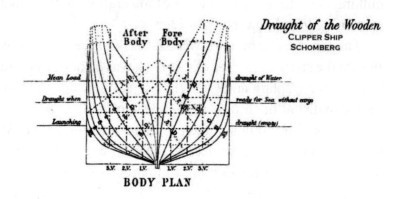

Halls had completed the basic structure of the *Schomberg* in April 1855, and she was formally launched. As she slipped into the Aberdeen harbour, nearby ships fired their guns in salute, and a crowd of an estimated 20,000 onlookers cheered loudly. She was towed to the adjacent Victoria Dock. Over the following weeks, the builders added her masts and rigging.

At the April 1855 launch, Alexander Hall & Sons held a banquet for 400 people. Among attendees representing Baines were Mr. Thomas Mackay, and other representatives, Mr. Harrison, a junior partner, and Captain

---

[30] The article from British news was reprinted in various Australian newspapers, including "Schomberg" *Empire* 10 Oct 1855 p.4
[31] https://babel.hathitrust.org/cgi/pt?id=mdp.39015004516913&view=1up &seq=201&skin=2021 accessed 12.10.2022

Forbes. Forbes had been in Aberdeen to oversee the finer details of the build. His father in Aberdeen had not been well and passed away four weeks before the launch.

Most of those at the luncheon were important guests from Aberdeen and Liverpool. There were the usual toasts, and the guest speaker was Mr. Austen Henry Layard, the new Lord Rector of Marischal College and the University of Aberdeen. Mr. Layard christened the craft *Schomberg* in honour of Vice-Admiral Charles Frederick Schomberg, Royal Navy, the current Liverpool Land and Emigration Commissioner. Captain C.F. Schomberg was an examiner of merchant vessels carrying passengers overseas from Liverpool. He was also a customer of shipping companies like James Baines & Co. when the Commission contracted ships to send financially-assisted migrants to the colonies. Captain Schomberg was not present at the launch: he could not have been seen to support one shipping company over another. In choosing that vessel's name, it might be that Baines & Co. was currying favour with the Commission. Near the end of the luncheon, the Principal of Marischal College, Daniel Dewar, proposed a toast to Captain Forbes' health, and Forbes responded briefly. He said how honoured he felt to stand before the ladies and gentlemen of his native city. He continued: "*Though the last ship I commanded went like lightning, I intend to make the "Schomberg" go like greased lightning.*"[32]

On June 30, Forbes took the rigged ship from Aberdeen with a crew of 70 riggers and a large party of ladies and gentlemen connected to the vessel's owners. [33] They travelled north, over the north of Scotland, passing the

---

[32] "Launch of the Australia Clipper-Ship Schomberg, the Largest Ever Built in Britain" *Aberdeen Journal* 11 Apr 1855 p.9

[33] "Arrival of the Schomberg" *Tasmanian Daily News* 23 Oct 1855 p.3

Shetlands and Lewis and Harris of the Outer Hebrides. A lack of wind becalmed the vessel for four days, so the passengers went ashore at South Uist. They then touched the coast of Ireland for one person to disembark, and continued down the west coast of England to Liverpool. Here, the last details were carried out: the copper plating of the hull, fitting out the interior, including carpentry, painting, and upholstery.

The Black Ball vessels were painted in their standard colours - black for the exterior, white for the interior and blue along the waterways.[34]

The workmen had completed their tasks within a day or two of the *Schomberg*'s scheduled sailing. When Second Cabin passenger and diary-keeper James Hopkins went on board with his belongings on 3rd October, the painters were just finishing: there was still the smell of fresh paint. Early on Sunday, 6th October 1855, she left Liverpool, was towed down the River Mersey, and headed for the open seas and Melbourne.

---

[34] STAMMERS defines waterways as "Thick strakes of planking at the sides of the deck over the ends of the beams and inside the top timbers. They form a gutter to take off the water on deck through the scuppers (holes in the bottom of the bulwarks)." ibid p.493 The bulwark is an extension of the vessel's sides to prevent the sea washing over the decks and to stop men being swept overboard.

4: Great Circle Sailing

From Liverpool, the route taken by Captain Forbes and other fast-sailing captains of that decade, as a time-saver, was known as great circle sailing. By the 1850s, there were two accepted sailing pathways for British ships to reach Australia – the Admiralty route and the great circle route. The conventional approach of the British Admiralty involved a stop at Cape Town. Before this decade, ships sailing this route or something similar had taken months to arrive.

J.T. Towson was a scientist and examiner of candidates for Mate and Master Certificates in Liverpool. He encouraged Liverpool captains to take the great circle route to travel faster to Australia. Another theorist working to improve navigation on the other side of the northern hemisphere was Lieutenant Maury of the American Navy. He had researched the behaviour of the ocean currents and winds per season by studying the logbooks of many ship captains. The work of both men changed the theories of navigation. Towson's sailing plan involved captains in daily recalculating position and plotting a course along the apparently "circular" line. If the captain modified the route to avoid foul weather or icebergs or islands, it was known as composite circle sailing. Towson published tables to assist navigators in carrying out complicated mathematical calculations.

Since the Earth is not flat as usually shown in maps using a Mercator projection, it was clear that by travelling along an apparently curved route, but for the most part sailing in a straight direction around a round world, a ship could reach its journey's end in less time. The *Schomberg* took this relatively new circle sailing route from Liverpool to Melbourne, modifying the circle to avoid the highest southern latitudes and the Antarctic ice fields. Circular sailing to Australia involved travelling further south, into the latitudes we know as the Roaring Forties and the Furious Fifties, to pass north or south of the Kerguelen Islands in the southern Indian Ocean. The strong westerly winds in those latitudes were a bonus, driving sailing ships forward to their destination at speed.

The first Captain to attempt Towson's advocated route was Captain Godfrey, sailing the *Constance* with emigrants from Plymouth to South Australia. A newspaper estimated that he saved a month in sailing time. Captain Forbes was not the first to take this route. He may not have been the second, but he took Towson's advice when sailing in the *Marco Polo*, the *Lightning*, and the *Schomberg* to Melbourne, and other Black Ball captains followed suit.

Within a couple of decades, ships powered by steam-driven propellers, and the opening of the Suez Canal, made this great circle, the Clipper Route, obsolete. But it remains the shortest path to circle the globe and is followed by modern-day racing yachtsmen.

The *Schomberg* sailed south from Liverpool, toward Brazil. They sailed closer to the coast at Pernambuco, Brazil, than they intended, being pushed westward by the southeast trade winds. Forbes came on deck late at night to check on their progress. He growled, "Man, you are way off course," and took command. Once they reached their desired southerly extent, they progressed more or less along that parallel until the ship passed the obstacle of the Kerguelen Islands, which lie just north of 50 degrees South. These Islands were a signal to Forbes and others to turn toward the northeast. Sailing ships heading for the eastern Australian colonies would expect to reach the coastline between the Victorian-South Australian border and Cape Otway on the western edge of Bass Strait.

The clipper ships did seem to compete with one another: which ship was best, the biggest, which fastest? Newspapers described the various sailings and any competing captains' achievements as one would the running of a horse race. Even in the days of the *Titanic*, speed was the thing, plus the importance of preserving reputation, and the added pressure of a highly anticipated maiden voyage. Forbes was not the only captain in the Black Ball Line to strive for a fast passage. Competition among shipping companies demanded it. For Forbes, one reason would have been to meet his employers' claims and expectations and sustain the high regard of the citizens in his home town Aberdeen. In his speech at the launch of the *Schomberg*, Mr. James Hall of Alexander Hall & Sons said that their customers, shipping companies, had seen how fast the railways in Britain had enabled personal travel and transport by rail. Now when shipping companies asked them about a ship, instead of asking first how much will it cost, they asked how fast she would go.[35]

~

---

[35] "Launch of the Australia Clipper-Ship Schomberg, the Largest Ever Built in Britain" op. cit.

Thomas Mackay of the Black Ball Line had earlier in that luncheon called for a toast "for a voyage of 60 days, and Forbes, the fastest man of the age."[36] Behind the goal of 60 days might have been the very lucrative British Post Office mail contract to carry the Australian post for which Baines was about to tender.

When the *Schomberg* reached Moonlight Head, Forbes would have remembered being delayed at this spot in 1852. In his first sailing of the *Marco Polo* to Melbourne, the vessel was within sight of Cape Otway when she could not move forward. It took another six days before they passed through Port Phillip Heads.[37] And then the Pilot managed to run the ship on a sandbank just inside the Heads.

~

Forbes may have been anxious not to ruin his reputation in Aberdeen, but by the time he returned from Melbourne, his reputation was indefinitely lost around the maritime world. What happened in the *Schomberg* during this sailing from Liverpool to Melbourne?

---

[36] ibid.
[37] MACGREGOR op. cit. p.188

5: Passage from Liverpool to Melbourne

Fortunately, three passengers kept shipboard diaries during the *Schomberg*'s maiden voyage to Australia: one by Thomas Angove, another by James Hopkins, and the last by Angelo Crotch Palmer. These personal records make reasonable sources to discover how the travellers found the journey and the events. While the three writers may not have witnessed everything on board, passengers in close accommodation did gossip. The copies of these diaries that have been made available to the public are incomplete. They are different, one from another, but together they provide a comprehensive picture. Several diaries from other passengers in south-bound vessels during this decade, when read, showed the commonalities in what life was like under sail.

~

The first of the diaries[38] was written by Thomas Angove, aged 33, from a Cornish-born mining family. Thomas came out to Victoria to manage the Clunes and Blackwood mining company in Victoria. His younger brother John

---

[38] ANGOVE *Diary of Thomas Angove*. Unpublished 1855 held by the State Library of Victoria

accompanied him. Thomas wrote his diary no doubt expecting just friends and family would read it, and he recorded scathing comments about the other travellers. But he often watched the daily readings of position, noted distances covered, and when the sails were put up or taken down. Thomas also observed Forbes as commander on deck in tricky situations. On one occasion, in a storm, Forbes' voice boomed, Thomas thought, loud enough to make the wind lie flat on the water.

The second diarist, James Hopkins, wrote daily about social happenings on board.[39] He began his notes when leaving home, bidding his friends and associates farewell, making his way by horse and cart to the station, then rail to Birmingham, and Liverpool. James was on board the *Schomberg* with his brother John, his cousin Ned Hopkins, cousin Matilda Edwards, and his uncle George Kelson in the Second Cabin. In the First Cabin was George's son, Mr. Isaac Hopkins Kelson, with his new wife: all of these belonging to the same extended family, the Hopkins of Wotton Under Edge, Gloucestershire.[40] When they reached Melbourne, the brothers, for some reason, went their own way. John went to Bendigo. James went to the diggings near Beechworth, taking a job in a hotel, one with a ballroom, in Sebastopol, along the Woolshed Creek, northwest of Beechworth. Once Hopkins had reached Sebastopol, he walked into the scrub and shed a few quiet tears, probably shocked by the loneliness of his new surroundings. By 1857 some 20,000 people were in the Beechworth area, searching for gold. Today this lovely

---

[39] HOPKINS, James *Emigrant's Journal of his Voyage from Liverpool to Australia*. Unpublished 1855 held by the State Library of Victoria.
[40] *England and Wales Census 1841 and 1851 in FamilySearch,* and information contained in James Hopkins' diary.

town's population is about 15% of that figure.

First Cabin passenger Angelo Palmer had sailed to and from Australia once before. His *Schomberg* diary was short and mainly talked about his travelling companions and how they entertained themselves playing guitar or playing cards or quoits, with a wager on each game. As a student of the law, Angelo also spent time reading various legal texts and other academic works.[41]

All travellers had come on board the *Schomberg* the night before sailing. James Hopkins noted the spectacle of Liverpool at night, under gas light. They weighed anchor at 6 a.m. on Sunday October 6, and proceeded down the River Mersey with the aid of a steam tug. Being very early in the morning, the *Schomberg* departed without fanfare, no cannons or guns fired, no tunes from bands. The surgeon examined the passengers to reduce the risk of disease aboard.

It seems the three diaries described what was, in effect, a typical passage in a sailing ship from Liverpool to Melbourne in the mid-nineteenth century. Like in other sailing ships, the working crew of the *Schomberg* came from several countries, being English, French, Spanish, Italian, Swedish, Irish, Scottish, and Chinese. Some of the passengers had a moment of regret, "what have I done," it was a momentous decision to travel so far to an unknown future. Their tug pulled away, breaking that last tie with home. As the *Marco Polo* departed from Liverpool two years earlier, in 1853, ships in the Mersey nearby fired their guns in salute, wishing those on board a safe passage. The German band aboard the *Marco Polo* played a current, heart-rending song, which made the passengers tearful as

---

[41] PALMER, Angelo Crotch *Diary* and *Letters* 1855-56. Unpublished, held by the Hamilton Historical Society.

they waved to those on shore, perhaps for the last time.[42]

In the evening of October 8, the steam tug that had aided the *Schomberg* down the Mersey left the ship to take herself further out to sea. Then the usual business of shipboard life began. The passengers formed into small dining groups known as messes. The ship's Purser each week distributed provisions from which each mess arranged their meals, which the galley crew would then cook.

In the same week as the *Schomberg*'s sailing, the British Parliament's amended *Passengers Act* came into force. The law now required captains and shipping companies to ensure their sailings adhered to the following regulations:

- Protection of passengers from tricksters and unscrupulous agents when arranging their passage and waiting for their ship to sail.
- Room on board ships for a hospital. Sailings with numbers of passengers over a distance must have a surgeon aboard.
- Space for passengers to exercise.
- Captain to record births, marriages, and deaths and give the cause of death.
- Pure water, wholesome provisions. The Purser might supply specified substitutes for some of the food items.
- Carry fewer passengers per voyage, no numbers near 800 or 1,000: crowded conditions facilitated the spread of disease.
- Sufficient crew.
- Fire engines (not as we know them, but a means of putting out fires).

---

[42] GREENHALGH op. cit. In CHARLWOOD, Don *Long Farewell.* Burgewood Books, Warrandyte, Vic. several editions 1981-2015.

- Lifeboats in appropriate numbers,
- and adequate ventilation to all decks.

Emigration Officers in Liverpool and other ports examined the ships and provisions and issued a certificate before sailing was permitted. The English officials had addressed the issue of passengers' welfare after the immigration officers in Victoria reported that four vessels had arrived in Port Phillip with unhealthy government-assisted migrants. These ships were the *Bouruduf*, the *Wanata*, the *Marco Polo*, and the *Ticonderoga*, which carried 752, 791, 960, and 800 passengers, each with dozens of deaths, mainly among young children.

The Melbourne commissioners reported that these ships, on the whole, were well-managed, clean, and orderly. Still, improvements were needed, better toilets, improved galleys, more spacious accommodation, dedicated ships' hospitals, and additional medical equipment and supplies. Small children were much more likely than adults to contract whooping cough, diphtheria, and measles. The adults were already survivors of these infectious diseases. In 1852 the *Ticonderoga* arrived at Port Phillip Heads with scarlet fever and measles aboard, flying the obligatory yellow flag. Several dozen individuals had already died at sea. Health inspectors redirected the vessel across Port Phillip Bay to the distant Point Nepean, and officials constructed a temporary quarantine station. The *Lysander*, the Victorian government hospital ship, anchored close by to assist. Altogether, a shocking number of 170 persons from the *Ticonderoga* lost their lives. Inspectors placed the *Bouruduf* in quarantine at Point Henry, Geelong. The *Wanata* came with typhus, *Marco Polo* with dysentery, measles, and whooping cough. Inspectors isolated them in quarantine. The Government later built a permanent quarantine facility at Point Nepean.

The recommendations from the Victoria health officials to the English Land and Emigration Commissioners included fewer persons per sailing, reduced numbers of children, and no crowding. With space and improved ventilation, diseases such as measles or scarlet fever would be more manageable. When the *Schomberg* was ready to sail, all the new requirements were in place. Although built to carry 1,000 persons, her number on board at departure was around 490, plus the crew.

On October 21, a couple of weeks into the trip, Thomas Angove, in his diary, wrote, "*our ship is gallantly spinning along. The old Admiral Schomberg still points the way, and as yet he has not moved the telescope from under his arm although I think he must have washed his face on the night we carried off the main degallant mast, We have no less than 32 sails spread on different masts. There is not a ship afloat that carries so much canvas.*"

Angove in his diary noted many of the sails in use, and from that information, the *Schomberg* at sea in full sail might have looked like the image on the following page.

~

For most passengers, the start of their trip would be something unfamiliar, the ship's rolling, with people unsteady on their feet until they developed their sea legs. While they adjusted to the wallowing of the craft, there was seasickness of varying degrees for many, but after a few days, most individuals were quite well.

1. Flying jib 2. Outer jib
3. Inner jib 4. Fore
topmast staysail
5. Foresail 6. Fore
topsail 7. Fore degallant
8. Fore royal 9. Fore
skysail
10. Mainsail 11. Main
topsail 12. Main
degallant
13. Main royal 14. Main
skysail 15. Mizzen sail
or Crossjack 16. Mizzen
topsail 17. Mizzen
degallant 18. Mizzen
royal 19. Mizzen skysail
20. Spanker
21-26. staysails named
for the mast to which
they attach
27-32. perhaps the
studding sails, added to
extensions to the ends of

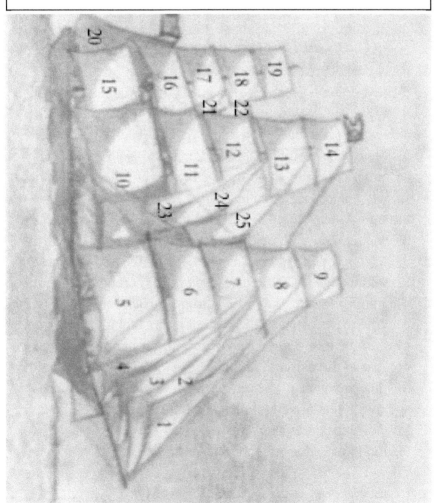

39

Sailing against the clock or calendar to achieve short voyages meant a ship left Liverpool carrying enough food to last months, not planning to stop at any port to refresh supplies. It would seem the food below decks in all ships was not great. It was salty meat and potatoes, "preserved" potatoes, which weren't particularly good. The *Marco Polo*, in 1853, with 648 paying passengers, took on board in Liverpool food in these quantities: 40 tons of fresh beef, 60 pigs, 40 sheep, 100 dozen fowls, five dozen geese, five dozen turkeys - 400 barrels of flour, etc.[43] Some passengers carried a few food items with them at embarkation in Liverpool. Those who hadn't brought such things as cake, pickled onions, cheese, sardines, jam, or ham, had regrets.

When the deck was awash in the first week at sea in the *Schomberg,* the crew and some Second Cabin passengers had seawater wetting their bedding and belongings. The accommodation for both groups lay toward the bow of the vessel. The carpenters plugged the hawse holes - the pipes through which the chains would pass when the crew cast the anchors. James Hopkins wrote about one occasion when the sea poured in through the portholes of the Seconds' area. He said that shoes and other goods floated around the floor. Captain Forbes sent a bottle of rum to each mess that had been flooded: "very considerate of him," thought James.

Turbulent and high seas occurred throughout voyages, not just in the extreme latitudes. The *Schomberg*'s draught (displacement of water) at the bow was 21 feet 6 inches, and aft 24 feet 6 inches when she left Liverpool.[44] In many sailing ships, seawater washed over the decks when in mountainous seas, entered the hatchways, and found its

---

[43] "Departure of the Marco Polo for Australia" 25 Mar 1853 *John O'Groat Journal* p.4
[44] STAMMERS op. cit. pp. 411-12

way down to the ship's lower levels. Manually operated pumps could remove excess water in the vessel and return it to the ocean. When the weather improved, passengers brought their wet bedding into the fresh air to remove any dampness.

From the start of the journey, the *Schomberg* mostly sailed through calm, fine weather. But as the vessel approached the equatorial waters, she was becalmed for days. It took 28 of the promised 60 or 65 days for them to reach the equator. Some sailing ships were becalmed in this region for even longer. Rachel Henning wrote in 1861 in a shipboard letter that her ship, the massive screw-driven steamship *Great Britain,* flew along in these latitudes, passing wind-powered ships that "lolled about with their sails flapping." The one disadvantage to coal-powered vessels was that your clothes became dirty with soot.[45]

There was not much to be done in ships under sail to progress when the winds dropped. In baffling winds, light winds that came from one point and then another, or winds that came head-on, ships would be tacked to and fro. The sailors worked the ship, slowly taking a zig-zag path in great sweeps across the sea, redirecting the sails, loosening ropes and hauling on others, trying to catch wind in the sails. But at other times, when strong winds came from the right direction, behind the sails, with plenty of canvas on the yardarms, a ship could rocket along, albeit with some discomfort, perhaps fear for some passengers. The clippers were built for just this, to catch the wind. They coped less well when the wind came head-on.

Almost every diary one might read contains complaints from the Seconds and Thirds about the food. The stewards

---

[45] HENNING, Rachel *Letters of Rachel Henning.* Several editions including Penguin Books, Ringwood, Vic. 1988.

served better meals to the Firsts, to those who had paid most for their tickets. They were more likely to have fresh meat. The Firsts enjoyed alcohol at dinner, and stewards attended their tables. Some Second Cabin passengers were disappointed in the provisions they received. But others seemed to have expected just what they got. In Michael Stammers' book, *Passage Makers*, he includes an image of a James Baines and Company's Intermediate cabin passenger's ticket for travel to Melbourne in the Black Ball's ship *Donald McKay* in 1857. The passenger was Margaret McLaughlin. She paid 17 GB pounds.[46]

In the body of the ticket was printed in detail the dietary allowance per adult per week, and the substitutes that the captain and purser may provide, e.g., preserved meat for salt pork or beef; molasses for sugar; coffee or chocolate for tea; currants for raisins; and mixed pickles for vinegar. The luggage allowance was ten cubic feet per statute adult. Mess utensils and bedding to be brought on board by the passengers.

In 1904 a Sydney newspaper published as an item, under the title "Old Times," a Black Ball advertisement from July 1854 which listed ten forthcoming sailings and ships' and captains' names. The price of passage with provisions but without alcohol was given as 50 pounds for First, 30 pounds for Second, 22 pounds for Intermediate, and 18 guineas for Third, with children under 14 years of age at half-price.[47] In 1850 an agricultural labourer's annual income was about 23 pounds.[48] His wife could earn half that amount. Many in

---

[46] STAMMERS op. cit. p.273

[47] "Old Times: From the Papers of Fifty Years Ago" *Evening News* (Sydney) 16 Jul 1904 p.2

[48] https://historyofwages.blogspot.com/2011/02/agricultural-labourers-wages-1850-1914.html accessed 31 Jul 2022

steerage were well-behaved, good people who could not afford a higher price for the journey, especially if a man was accompanied by his wife and children. Occasionally Second and Third passengers complained to the Purser about the food. One Second Cabin passenger in the *Schomberg,* Mr. Melville, on November 1, tangled with the Purser, who came down to the Second Cabin to talk about the beef, and the two had "very high words." The Purser threatened to break Melville's back, and in return, Melville said he would knock the Purser's head off. Thomas Angove had noted of Mr. and Mrs. Melville, although they travelled in Second Class, one could tell that they had moved in elevated circles in their past life, nothing suited them.

About halfway through any journey, all passengers had grown tired of each other and everything else. On any ship, as people became bored, a few took to squabbling, engaged in petty arguments, insulted each other, "had words," some were quick to take umbrage, thin-skinned as they say. Some drank too much and even got into fist fights. The Firsts on some ships were sometimes as bad as the rest. One diary tells us that a disagreement at the card table in the Firsts led to the men drawing their pistols. Other migrants peacefully spent time together on the deck, talking, sewing, or singing. Songs they all knew were songs from church. One song they mentioned was the "old One Hundred":

> "All people that on earth do dwell,
> Sing to the Lord with cheerful voice:
> Him serve with mirth, His praise forth tell:
> Come ye before Him and rejoice."[49]

In most emigrant ships, well-attended religious services were held at least once a week, sometimes twice on a

---

[49] KETHE, William "All People That on Earth do Dwell", 1561

Sunday. In the *Schomberg*, these were led by First Cabin passenger Reverend Ross and occasionally by others. When the evenings were fine, there was dancing on the deck with music. A small German band played the dance music in the *Schomberg*, including the "Schomberg Galop" [sic], a musical piece written for this new craft. The passengers also danced the "Polka," the "Schottische," and "Sir Roger de Coverly."

To relieve passengers' boredom, the Officers organized entertainment. There were balls, fancy dress, lots of card games, and on occasion, invitations for Second Cabin passengers to attend an event in the Firsts' saloon. Some First Cabin passengers contributed and performed items to interest others for their enjoyment. Some learned men gave lectures on subjects in the *Schomberg*, such as "poetry and astronomy" "the pleasure of intellectual freedom." They occasionally staged mock trials; passengers turned actors, judge and jury, with melodramatic themes, like a breach of promise, to make everyone laugh, no doubt a lawyer or two among them to advise.

Only the First Cabin passengers were permitted to keep their guns. They shot at and sometimes killed birds that came near, even the fantastic albatross: they fired at porpoises and sharks. All ships passed whales and many kinds of fish; at times, there was fluorescence in the dark sea, or they saw the spectacle of flying fish leaping out of the water; they encountered the odd turtle, even a nautilus swimming along.

While becalmed in the equatorial zone, the heat and stifling air were unbearable. In the *Schomberg*, and likely in many other ships, the temperature reached 100 degrees Fahrenheit on the hottest days. Some passengers slept on deck. Occasionally the crew arranged sea bathing, taking a few people in a small boat a short distance from the ship so that they might jump into the water. On the earlier trip in 1853 of the *Marco Polo*, one man taking such a dip died, witnesses said, of sunstroke, within fifteen minutes' exposure. But passenger Edwin Bird wrote that the man had swallowed a lot of seawater and had been drinking alcohol all morning.[50]

Away from the tropical doldrums, with a good wind in her sails, the *Schomberg* was fast, caught up with, and passed slower vessels, despite her weighty cargo. A poem or chanty, perhaps written by Cicely Fox Smith, shows how seamen viewed their leviathans wrestling with nature in the windy, extreme latitudes.

"Crack her on with all she'll carry,
What she can't, she'll have to drag!"
Was the way they used to work things
Underneath the Black Ball flag . . .

When it was "Blow, bullies, blow,
On a Circle southward ho!
You can let her rip — she's a Liverpool ship,
And you bet she's bound to go!" [51]

Now and again, they encountered a friendly vessel, perhaps passing on its way back to England. Many on board enjoyed a great evening when the *Schomberg* met a sister Hall-built ship, the *Vision*, taking tea home from China. Her captain was another Scot, well known to Forbes. A small boat carried Captain Douglas between the two ships. Douglas and Forbes spent time in conversation over a meal,

---

[50] BIRD, Edwin *Diary 1853* Unpublished, 1853.
[51] SMITH, Cicely Fox "Liverpool Ship" in *Full Sail: More Sea Songs and Ballads*, Houghton Mifflin Co., New York, 1926, pp.111-113.

followed by celebrations and music, and both Captains danced with passengers on deck. When the vessels separated, the *Vision* carried about 500 letters from the *Schomberg* folk back to England.[52] It was the custom for any ship sighting another to report her to the newspapers on arriving in port. The information was published under the heading "spoken for". Hopefully, if a vessel was missing, like the *Guiding Star*, another ship had recorded her last position.

Many travellers spent lots of their time on deck, in the fresh air, watching the waves crashing about, sending sprays of water into the sunlight, which turned the mist into coloured sparkles. Some nights the sunsets were amazing. Other nights, those on deck saw great darkness with no moon or a sliver of a moon, peeping out from behind dark, solid clouds. They watched the endless ocean and the overarching sky and were amazed as clouds rushed past. They observed a changing display of stars between the hemispheres, millions of them glittering in the deep darkness. Some missed the familiar stars of the northern hemisphere and didn't think much of the Southern Cross.

As they travelled further south, the days and nights became extremely cold. Sometimes the noise and the rolling and weaving of the ship kept passengers below decks, in bed, where at least they found some warmth. In some ships, there might be hanging baskets of burning coals. Occasionally, those on board started an accidental fire, perhaps by a careless smoker, a hidden oil lamp at bedtime, or by the cooks in the galley. A lad almost caused a fire in one ship by tossing lit papers around near his family's belongings. In one ship, a lady managed to catch

---

[52] "Schomberg" *Age* February 27th, 1856 p. 2

her hat on fire. Safety in wooden ships at sea depended on a quick reaction.

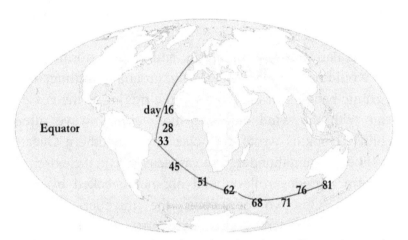

Schomberg's Route Showing the Number of Days Passed Since Departure

This image is based on a Hammer projection[53] and gives an idea of *Schomberg*'s route. Without wind, they lost days across the equatorial region. Eventually, they moved forward. The third mate was on duty late at night on day 33 when Forbes came on deck and said, "Man, you are way off course." The trade winds had driven the vessel far too close to Pernambuco, Brazil. The ship's progress in the days 45 to 74 in the higher southern latitudes was quick, thanks to the strong prevailing westerly winds. The final week of the passage saw them suffer again from lack of wind or a headwind. On day 16, they glimpsed San Antonio Island of the Cape Verde group, then passed the longitude of the Prince Edward Islands on day 62, and passengers saw the

---

[53] Based on the Hammer projection of the globe courtesy of Free World Maps, https://www.freeworldmaps.net/printable/ accessed 17.2.2022

Kerguelen Islands on day 68.

~

As they sailed further south, the wind howled, and heavy waves thumped into the ship's side, shivering the timbers. It became achingly cold, and the cold caused chilblains. There might be sleet in the wind, flurries of stinging hail or snow, lightning, and terrific storms. The ship would be noisy, with creaking, groaning, rattling, and rhythmic banging of the blocks in the rigging as the vessel dealt with the wind and one mountainous wave after another. Hopkins wrote the noise in the Southern Ocean was like constant thunder. The vast seas here in the extreme southern latitudes roll on and on, not checked by any continent. On two occasions, the travellers in the *Schomberg* came across massive icebergs which they sailed towards but kept from at some distance. One was likened to a marble mountain, rising 100 feet out of the sea. Neither Hopkins nor Angove feared their closeness and were amazed by the experience.

~

In gales or stormy conditions, sailing ships suffered damage: a broken section of a mast, sails ripped by the wind, or a sail came crashing down to the deck. Like other captains of the clipper era, Forbes pushed his vessels hard, so there was plenty of work for the ships' carpenters and the sailmakers. On the evening of November 13, the breeze had strengthened. As the Captain ordered, the *Schomberg* crew took in the mizzen degallant, royal, and skysails, made one reef in the mizzen topsail, hauled up the mizzen sail, took a reef in the mainsail, leaving them with the main top, main degallant, foresail, foretop, and fore degallant. Heavy rain came at around 9.30 the following morning, and then the wind suddenly turned around. "*The Captain was on*

48

deck for several hours with the rain pouring on him like a torrent, with nothing on him but Chinese trousers and a shirt, no hat or shoes on his feet...The ship had barely been put to rights by midnight, and then we were close-hauled," wrote Thomas Angove.

~

During the night of December 11, they passed at a distance the rugged group of Kerguelen Islands. The main island was in sight but not close. Nevertheless, they passed along scattered reefs with surf breaking over them. Angove enjoyed watching the energetic Captain Forbes bounding around the deck like a kangaroo, shouting a thousand commands in his Scottish accent, one after another. These Kerguelen islands were known to Forbes, but he may not have known that the islets and reefs extended far and wide when he sailed sooner than expected among them during the hours of darkness in the *Lightning* in 1854.[54] In these regions, captains could experience some days together where the reckoning of position could not occur due to poor weather.

From the Kerguelens, the *Schomberg* took a new heading, northeast towards the Victorian coast. By the following day, she was again subject to unhelpful winds, almost becalmed. The crew brought up the anchor chains from below. Four days later, on Christmas Day, land was sighted near Cape Bridgewater, close to Portland in far western Victoria.

Faced with a headwind, the crew of the *Schomberg* tacked back and forth repeatedly to catch wind or a breeze from the right direction to see them move forward to Port Phillip. Angelo Palmer wrote that each time they tacked

---

[54] FENWICK, John *Diary 1854* In CHARLWOOD, Don *Long Farewell* Burgewood Books, Reprinted 2005 pp. 227-249.

they gained just a matter of inches: a very frustrating time for the men working the ship and, no doubt, the passengers keen to get to Melbourne. Eventually they sighted Moonlight Head. Late at night on Boxing Day, they found themselves some 30 miles back to the west of Moonlight Head. The distance made good was only 60 or so miles after 33 hours from their first sight of land at Cape Bridgewater. Had the winds come from a better direction they might have reached Port Phillip Heads within a day. This was not to be. Forbes took the ship in close to shore in the hope of finding a local offshore breeze: the warm land of summer cools after sunset and the wind then flows offshore. Such a breeze did eventuate, but a current running to the northwest caused the clipper to continually drift in until it was too close to the shore and the ship ran aground. Two and a half days later the vessel was abandoned.

~

Captain Forbes on his way to Melbourne, aboard the coastal steamer *Keera*, explained the order of events to others. His words were reported in the *Argus*.[55] The vessel was on the starboard tack, out of sight of land, some distance east of Newfield Bay. When he estimated they were four or five miles from shore he ordered prepare to 'bout ship.[56] The wind was falling, there was a southerly swell on the sea. They attempted to tack but the ship missed stays, did not obey the helm. The crew measured the depth of the sea by heaving the lead and found it to be 17 fathoms [112 feet]. They then wore ship, tried to turn in the opposite direction so a breeze might push them around. The wind was freshening. Mr. Saxby, the Officer of the watch, reported

---

[55] "Wreck of the Schomberg" *Argus* 2 Jan 1856 p.4
[56] 'bout ship: to go from one tack to another, turning the ship's head into the wind

later in court that an offshore breeze had sprung up and was pushing the ship around.[57]

Forbes' account continued: all sail was ordered and the vessel came around easily and was headed south by east by the compass when she tailed onto the reef. The lead cast again revealed a sea depth of just 4 fathoms [24 feet]. A boat was lowered, and it was then they discovered that there was a coastal current running to the northwest, at a speed of three or four knots an hour. This current was not marked in Forbes' chart, although local steamer captains were aware of it. After two hours the ship's head had swung around to face the shore.

The image on the next page is of an artwork by N. [Nathaniel] Whittock, "City of Melbourne", about 1855, courtesy of the State Library of Victoria. The first Victorian train line, Melbourne to Sandridge Pier, now Port Melbourne, is shown here. Note the many dozens of smaller ships anchored in the River Yarra, alongside various warehouses.

---

[57] Angelo Palmer, in one of his letters back to England, January 1856, wrote that an officer told him they were looking for a wind which would come off the land.

6: *Schomberg* Lost: Forbes' Reception in Melbourne

Briefly, the vessel was caught on submerged rocks late on December 26, 1855, 81 days after leaving Liverpool. The crew was unable to refloat her. Mr. Millar and Mr. Dixon, both passengers, with crew members, took a lifeboat to sea. They searched for a landing place, unsuccessfully. Somehow, in the dark but, it was said, moonlit night, they missed the nearby broad sandy beach. Crew members fired guns and rockets to signal any passing ship of their plight. As it happened, a coastal steamer heading west to Portland saw their blue flare and approached. The following morning, rowers in lifeboats, led by Mr. Millar, moved passengers from the stricken vessel to board this coastal steamer, the *Queen*. She turned back to the port of Melbourne and delivered the Australian mail and the *Schomberg* passengers. The Hobson's Bay Railway Company ran a free train for these travellers, taking them from the port into the heart of Melbourne. Once there, restauranteur, Mr.Tilke, laid on a complimentary breakfast for one or two hundred hungry passengers who crowded around his door in Bourke Street.

~

The news of the stranding of the *Schomberg* having reached Melbourne, authorities sent several coastal steamers to the area then known as Curdies River: the *Queen, Champion, Marion, Keera,* and *Lioness.* The *Keera* was at the wreck on the Saturday in the early evening. The crew loaded the passengers' luggage and some cargo items into the *Keera* as she lay alongside the *Schomberg.* The sea began to rise. The *Keera* moved away and "kept in the offing all night." The bulk of the crew members headed by the Boatswain declared the wreck unsafe and rowed themselves to the beach, taking some food and rum with them. Those left behind on the *Schomberg* were six seamen, four stewards, the First and Second Mates plus Forbes and Captain Matthews, the local agent for Lloyd's of London. Overnight the sea was breaking over the wreck. The *Queen* arrived in the morning with James Baines & Co.'s local shipping agent, a stevedore and 20 men. The *Lioness* arrived. The steamers left the scene when the forceful sea washed all items on deck overboard.[58] One side of the vessel was now underwater.

~

Shortly after the steamer *Queen* had delivered the passengers to Melbourne, the newspapers began reporting shocking rumours. The stories caught the interest of the general population of Melbourne. By the time Captain Forbes arrived in town, one paper had said while hesitating to print such malicious reports as the ones they were hearing, there were indeed questions that Forbes needed to answer. One letter to a newspaper Editor said Forbes had given assurances that the voyage would only last 65 days. The letter ended by saying it was necessary to wait to

---

[58] "Wreck of the Schomberg" *Argus* 2 Jan 1856 p.4

confirm all the facts.[59] Another writer simply called for punishment. A *Melbourne Herald* article asked the question, "*Why was the Schomberg so near the shore? We do not, of course presume to impute blame to Captain Forbes. We are at present not sufficiently well informed, to justify us in doing so. But it is impossible to prevent men from asking the above question.*"[60]

The sources relied on by the author to determine the facts were the witness depositions that clerks took down to prepare for the court hearings, Captain Forbes' accounts, various articles in the newspapers, eye-witness testimonies, James Hopkins' diary, and Angelo Palmer's letters home. Thomas Angove's diary ended before they reached Cape Bridgewater and Portland.

~

Various agencies provided immediate help for passengers without friends or family in Melbourne. The Government instructed the Immigration Agent to assist the passengers at their depot and provide them with provisions for a few days. The amended *Passengers Act* of the U.K. 1855 entitled passengers to remain with their ship once at its destination for 48 hours. The local agent for the Black Ball Line also asked passengers to call at their office in Melbourne for assistance and advised that James Baines & Co. would contribute some relief funds for lost luggage. A refuge named the Immigrants' Home lay on the eastern side of the Prince's Bridge over the River Yarra.

The first reports of the loss of the ship in the Melbourne newspapers were sympathetic and gave thanks there had been no loss of life. The *Argus* newspaper printed a version

---

[59] NAUTICUS "Loss of the Schomberg" *Empire* (Sydney) January 3, 1856 p.5
[60] "Schomberg's End" *Melbourne Herald* 1 Jan, 1856

of events as told by two old colonists, whose account was similar to Forbes'. They said the Captain attempted to 'bout ship and wear ship. The vessel had almost passed the line of breakers when she ran upon rocks. The men said Forbes was "cool and collected." He immediately sent a boat to look for a landing and prepared the other longboats. These old colonists thought the tragedy occurred because Forbes was not familiar with the strength of the current at this place and because the breeze fell away at a most critical moment.[61]

It was December 28 when the passengers reached Melbourne by the *Queen*. That same day, the President of the Chamber of Commerce was visited by a group of men from the *Schomberg* and agreed to call a Special Meeting of the Chamber for the following morning. They would discuss the losses suffered by passengers.

The *Geelong Advertiser and Intelligencer* reported a wharf-side meeting in Melbourne on January 2nd. A party of passengers met to determine how to publicise their grievances and devise measures to obtain redress. Those at the meeting had appointed a secretary to draw up their arguments. Those men involved had not made this meeting public, so it had almost escaped the notice of the press, the article said.[62]

When Forbes reached Melbourne, he immediately wrote to the newspapers to explain how the *Schomberg* was lost. In his letter, he said the same as he had in conversation in the *Keera*. But he also stated emphatically that the anchors were ready to be deployed at the time of the disaster.[63] This

---

[61] "Wreck of the Schomberg. All on Board Saved" *Argus* 29 Dec, 1855 p.4.
[62] "Melbourne" *Geelong Advertiser* 3 Jan, p.2
[63] "Wreck of the Schomberg" *Argus* 4 Jan, 1856 p.4

was untrue.

In the handful of days after the passengers reached Melbourne, the wild stories published in the press had been enlarged and had greatly excited the citizens of the town. On the same day, the morning papers noted an advertisement, placed by the Chamber of Commerce, of a meeting of passengers by the *Schomberg* to take place that morning.[64] The purpose of the Passengers Meeting was to investigate the alleged disgraceful conduct of Captain Forbes and Officers of the ship and recover monies lost by passengers, presumably including local merchants who had lost their imported stocks. Of the passengers, most of those who travelled in First Cabin, about 60 adults and children, were known to be returning citizens. Just 12 were coming to Melbourne for the first time.[65] Those who spoke up at the Public Meeting were one or two members of the crew and several passengers from the Second Cabin, plus Mr. Isaac Kelson and Mr. George Wharton from the First. Some of those present would have been merchants whose cargo was not insured. Insurance was certainly available. One man later said he had considered insuring his goods but thought the price too high.

Attendees gathered at the Mechanics Institute, Collins Street, in the building now known as the Athenaeum, on January 3rd. It was a riotous affair, with unsworn statements from the accusers. There were exclamations and interjections from the audience throughout the meeting, loud and hearty laughter, especially for the more salacious allegations. One journalist reported that it was possible to recognise that about half of those present were passengers;

---

[64] "Schomberg: Meeting of Passengers" *Argus* 3 Jan, 1856 p.4 and "Schomberg" *Age* 3 Jan, 1856 p.2
[65] "English Shipping" *Argus* 29 Dec, 1855 p.4

the rest were familiar faces, members of the public.[66] The Melbourne papers the following day described the proceedings and the resolutions passed. Here is a precis of the articles printed by the three major Melbourne newspapers:

Those assembled chose a Chairperson, Mr. Harker, a member of the Chamber of Commerce. A passenger from the First Cabin, Mr. Isaac Kelson, said everyone knew the Captain and the Doctor each had a woman in their cabin all day, every day, and well into the night. One of the "ladies" had been caught creeping back to her bunk at daylight, half-dressed!

Mr. Tinlen stirred the pot. He said he had seen one in bed with the Captain on St. Stephen's Day [Boxing Day]. Laughter came from the crowd. Mr. Tinlen's name does not appear in the list of passengers; perhaps he was a crew member or a passenger's servant and was not named in the Public Record Office of Victoria (PROV) list of those on board.[67]

Mr. Isaac Kelson had travelled in the First Cabin and objected to the two women being dined in the Firsts' saloon when nobody else from the Second Cabin had this privilege.

Mr. Melville moved the first resolution: the ships' Captain, Surgeon, and Officers were ungentlemanly, discourteous, tyrannical, and grossly immoral. Mr. Norris seconded the motion.

Mr. Fenn, a South Australian solicitor who travelled in the First Cabin, was present and spoke up; he said he

---

[66] "Public Meeting of the Passengers by the Schomberg" *Melbourne Herald* 4 Jan, 1856
[67] Public Record of Victoria. Unassisted Passenger Lists.

expected, given the seriousness of the charges read out in a public forum, that they should offer some evidence to justify the accusations.

Mr. Kelson spoke again and asked to amend the subjects of the first charge to just the Captain and the Surgeon and not the whole of the senior crew.

Mr. Melville, it was said, was treated discourteously when he complained to Forbes that even dogs would not eat the meat provided. [Doctor Hardy was present, and it was he who commented that some dogs had sensitive stomachs].

Mr. Carpenter said he knew of Forbes being down on the Irish crew. One time, he said, Forbes got them out of bed at 2.30 a.m. and put them in irons for 4 or 5 hours.

Mr. Godkin, a passenger, proposed the second resolution: Everyone present attributed the loss of the vessel to the gross negligence of the Captain. When the Officers warned Forbes that they were close to shore, "he was indulging himself with the ladies in his private cabin and could not come up to render assistance."

Mr. Johnson, a mariner and passenger, stated the Captain could have saved the *Schomberg* if he ordered an anchor to be dropped.

Mr. Williams, a passenger, told the meeting that he asked another man to wake the crew on duty, as they were asleep at the wheel when the ship was getting close to shore.

At one point during the meeting, a voice called for three cheers to the downfall of the Black Ball Line. The crowd's response indicated that he had gone too far.

Mr. Stockdale said the Captain was reckless and accused him of bravado. He questioned if Forbes intended to destroy the ship. He said the passengers saw land for an hour, but Forbes ordered 'bout ship just five minutes before they struck the reef.

Mr. Melville said the Captain, when told they were close to shore, had answered the *Schomberg* could go to Hell; they should call him when she was on the beach.

Mr. Carpenter moved the third resolution. Their tickets, contracts with James Baines and Co. entitled them to better quality and quantity of water and food. This agreement had not been honoured.

Mr. Tinlen called out; the crew killed the pigs for the table after they were already dead. Roars of laughter from the room.

Mr. Wharton from the First Cabin said the food and wine supplied by the Black Ball Line were substandard. He claimed that the stewards served only pork for six weeks to those in the First Cabin. The sherry was "infamous."

Mr. Connolly, Mr. Tinlen, and Mr. Stockdale proposed the fourth resolution, which Isaac Kelson seconded, and the vote was carried unanimously. A delegation should call on the Officer administering the Government to request an investigation of their claims. Governor Hotham of Victoria had died a couple of days earlier of cholera, hence the phrase the "Officer administering the Government."

Mr. John Millar proposed a vote of thanks to Captain Doran of the *Queen* for coming to them in their distress and returning to Melbourne to deliver the passengers from the *Schomberg*. (Captain Doran was later awarded 200 pounds.) Mr. Adams of the First Cabin seconded the motion. The meeting ended.[68]

It was essential to bring Captain Forbes and Officer of the watch, Mr. Saxby, before the courts as the losses to passengers had been substantial. The wreck would have

---

[68] Selected text from "Public Meeting of the Passengers by the Schomberg" *Melbourne Herald,* January 4, 1856 and "Loss of the Schomberg" *Argus* 4 Jan, 1856 p.1

been highly costly for Melbourne merchants. But those who had suffered losses could only take Forbes, Third Officer Saxby, or James Baines & Co. to court later for compensation if the Melbourne courts reached a guilty verdict. For Forbes, it was essential to discount the accusations if he was to clear his name.

Various individuals started writing to the newspapers. One paper said hundreds of letters had crossed their desks. They published just a sample of the letters received. Another newspaper defended the comments in the letters from those who were not mariners, saying they knew how to sail. They had come out by ship. Many of the letters were probably from passengers of the stricken vessel, but one cannot be sure since rarely did a letter-writer use his name: they signed as SUBSCRIBER, NAUTICUS, DAVY JONES, HEAVY SUFFERER, X, etc.

One writer or editor for the *Age* put together a lengthy article, blasting Forbes, and adding a moral judgment. The article, "Nautical Manners and Morality," said in part:

"Everybody who has had the misfortune to spend three or four months onboard a vessel commanded by a man of rude, surly, or brutal manners - addicted very much to the use of a blasphemous style of speech, - overbearing and insolent in his bearing towards the passengers and savagely tyrannical in his treatment of the crew, - will agree with us that those three or four months were about as wretched as any he ever spent in his life...In plain language, they are accused of making the Schomberg a brothel, and that in the most shameless way, - not covertly and quietly, but openly and in defiance of the good sense and good feelings of the passengers." [69]

---

[69] "Nautical Manners and Morals" *Age* 7 Jan, 1856 p.2

But another newspaperman wrote: "...*we shall look to the forthcoming inquiry. We do not think it fair to give currency to all the nonsense, and possibly mischievous invention, which vanity, or vexation, or officiousness of passengers, may have manufactured for the credulous. On all such occasions, we find a certain class of people, always ready with wonderful disclosures, and their worthlessness only appears with their cross-examination.*"[70]

Following the Passengers Meeting, Forbes and Saxby were charged and bailed. The first court hearing took place in the Williamstown District Police Court. The charges, or information, were laid by Mr. Broad, the Immigration Agent at Williamstown. The Magistrate on the Bench was Lieutenant Pascoe, R.N., and Melbourne lawyer Mr. Read argued for the Defence. [71] Written depositions or testimonies were to inform the proceedings of the Police Court and following Supreme Court. Those who provided written testimony were the *Schomberg* officers and crew, Henry Cooper Keen, First Officer; Jonathan Richard Saxby, Third Officer; Aubrey John Somerville, Fifth Officer; Samuel William Hardy, Surgeon; James Hodge, Boatswain; Lyndon Breen, carpenter; James Matheson, carpenter and Joseph Osbaldistone, Purser's Mate. The passengers who provided written statements were from the Second and Third Cabin: William Melville, Alexander Stockdale, James Paul, and Thomas Wilkinson. Others who testified were Daniel McIntosh of the British Hotel in Melbourne, and Barnard Robert Mathews, the local Lloyd's

---

[70] "Impartial, Not Neutral" *Melbourne Herald* 5 Jan, 1856
[71] "Schomberg" Argus 10 Jan 1856 p.5 and "Passengers by the Schomberg" *Age* 10 Jan, 1856 p.3

agent.[72]

Here is the gist of the written depositions from the crew, their versions of events: Third Officer Saxby said he was in charge of the watch on the night of December 26. They had reached Moonlight Head earlier in the day and could not move forward. They were tacking, searching for a favourable breeze. At the end of the evening, the ship was heading northwest on the starboard tack, close-hauled, with single reefed topsails and reefed top gallant sails. The land was out of sight. At about 9.30 p.m., Saxby saw the moon rise and could see a bank of fog. To check that it was not land, he called the Captain, who used his glass and ordered him to keep on the present tack. After ten minutes, he again thought he could see land. Forbes was walking about the deck, having been called by the Surgeon. He remained on deck.

First Officer Keen testified, both in written form and in person, that he, too, was on deck. The Captain was giving the orders. About 10 p.m., he ordered all hands 'bout ship. The entire crew had been on deck for the last 15 minutes, ready to carry out orders. What wind or breeze there was fell away. The action failed when the *Schomberg* did not obey the helm and missed stays: an unsuccessful attempt to turn. The next order was to wear ship, change heading relative to the breeze. When the vessel's head was almost around, facing out to sea, the ship's stern struck submerged rocks [at the eastern end of a reef in what is today Newfield Bay, adjacent to Curdies Inlet]. Both the watch, Mr. Saxby and First Mate Mr. Keen, believed they had plenty of room to manoeuvre.

---

[72] Public Record Office of Victoria. *James Nicol Forbes Neglect of Duty as Master of the British Ship Schomberg* VPRS 30/P0029, 2-160-29 1856-02-21

The crew did not immediately drop the anchor when they caught on the rock, as they hoped to move away from the reef. When this did not happen, the crew assembled the anchor, bent the cable to it in five or ten minutes, and the men cast it. Mr. Matheson, a carpenter, estimated it took him five minutes to remove the bung from the hawse-hole. Mr. Keen and Mr. Saxby thought ten had elapsed before the anchor was ready. Saxby and Keen did not believe dropping the anchor sooner would have saved the ship. The strong swell would have carried her onto rocks, regardless. Mr. Somerville, Fifth Mate, who also testified, agreed. Each surge of the sea heaved the vessel toward the beach.

Boatswain Hodge, in his deposition, claimed the crew did not drop the anchor for two and a half hours after hitting the rocks. Hodge himself would have dropped the anchor when she missed stays. From his experience from four sailings with Forbes, the Captain usually had the anchors ready three days before sighting land.

Passenger James Hopkins, in his diary, described hearing the ship strike against something and then general panic among the passengers. In particular, the ladies were fearful and in tears. But Hopkins wrote they were not in any great danger, and all could have been landed on the beach by lifeboats within an hour.

The grounding occurred very late on Thursday night. The Captain and Officers cut away the masts by mid-morning on Friday as the vessel was straining heavily against the swell. She had 20 ft of seawater in her hold and had already broken in half. By the Saturday, the weather had swung around and was coming from the southwest. When the men could not salvage additional luggage safely, they abandoned the ship. Captain Forbes, some crew, and passenger Mr. Palmer travelled on the last steamer coming to their aid before the sea was too rough for any other vessel to approach.

Some Officers remained on the beach near the wreck until the water and customs police secured everything ready for the official salvage auction. These Officers, crewmen, and the band members later walked 33 miles to Warrnambool, from where they took a coastal steamer to Melbourne. The newspaper from the nearest town reported several dozen men marched into Warrnambool, with the German shipboard band playing and leading the way.[73]

On the next page is a painting by Melbourne artist Philip J. Gray (1981), of the *Schomberg Aground*, caught on the reef, with a steamer attending. The original painting is held by Peterborough Residents Group.

---

[73] "Warrnambool" *Portland Guardian and Normanby Advertiser* 7 Jan, 1856 p.3

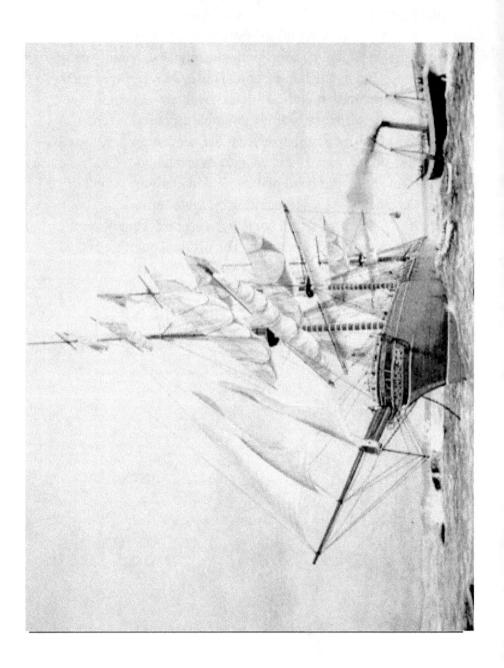

7: Court Hearings of the Charges Against Forbes

Two weeks after the wreck, the first court hearing took place in Williamstown. The District Police Court assembled on January 10th, 1856. Captain Forbes faced charges under the provisions of the *Passengers Act 1855* U.K., amended, which came into force on October 1, 1855. The first charge to be heard followed the complaints made by fifteen passengers of inferior provisions. Forbes' legal representative requested a postponement to enable Captain Forbes to have his officers present, some of whom were not yet in Melbourne. The Magistrate, Lieutenant Pascoe, perhaps wondering why Forbes was unprepared, asked when the court officer had served him his summons. Forbes replied he had not received one: this was not the truth. Forbes was served in the afternoon of the previous day. Forbes had looked at his watch and then torn the summons to pieces in front of the man.[74]

On January 14th, the coastal steamer *Champion* brought to Melbourne from Warrnambool the *Schomberg*'s Second Mate, the Purser, and 79 crew members.[75] The hearing in

---

[74] "Passengers by the Schomberg" *Age* 10 Jan, 1856 p.3
[75] "Shipping Intelligence" *South Australian Register* 17 Jan, 1856 p.2

Williamstown recommenced on January 17th. People crowded into the Court: the case had excited keen interest. The charges related to claims of less water being given on board than stipulated in the *Act*; poor quality of the food, especially the meat provided; the substitution of one food for another, such as molasses for sugar.

The hearing was exhausting, lasting the whole day. The evidence provided by witnesses was inconsistent and exceedingly trivial, said one journalist.[76] At the request of the defendant's counsel, all witnesses had been ordered out of Court so that they did not hear each other's testimony. Sixteen men aired complaints: ten Second and six Third Cabin passengers. Their complaints were inconsistent and contradictory, such as: the food is not as good as at home; I don't like oats, I don't like pork, the beef was tough, the beef was soft, the pork was fine. The ship ran out of sugar, and some passengers objected to treacle, molasses, as a substitute. Some preferred the treacle. Someone claimed they only received one type of meat, pork, for weeks.

One man said, when he complained, the Captain took him by the neck and ordered him to go downstairs. The man added, "what's the point of talking to a man who threatens to put you in irons." Another said, when he grumbled about the sugar and molasses, the Purser cut out his ration of lard. William Reid said he was an experienced traveller and had never had so much water before this sailing. Mr. Paul admitted when his wife and children were ill, they received soup from the Captain's table. Mr. Melville stated when his wife was sick, she received lamb chops for several days - but they were hardly worth eating, he said, all bone. The salted meat the cooks served seems to have stayed salty

---

[76] "Schomberg: Investigation at Williamstown" *Argus* 17 Jan,1856 p.5 continued *Argus* 19 Jan, 1856 p.5

even when cooked. One man testified he loved the pea soup: others didn't. The folk in the lowest deck existed on meals not much better than ham and pea soup. The galley crew gave everyone in the Seconds and Thirds hardtack as part of their diet – a biscuit of flour and water, for long-keeping baked hard, until not a skerrick of moisture remained. Mess members could grind these and use them as flour or dip them into tea or broth to soften. The hearing about provisions continued over to a second day. There was so much variance and contradiction among the statements about the water and the food that the Bench, Lieutenant Pascoe R.N. concluded he had no confidence in the evidence presented. The new *Passengers Act* allowed the substitution of one item for something similar. The charges were unproven, and Pascoe dismissed this part of the case.

There had been no shortage of water available to passengers. Each day the Fourth Mate kept a record of water given to passengers and then visited or sent for those who hadn't appeared. When the ship left Liverpool, they carried enough water per regulation for each person to last seven months. The food provided to the different classes on the *Schomberg* was no different from that given on other ships of the time. Only the First Cabin passengers were well fed.

The Williamstown Police Court hearing continued on January 19th and following days, examining the second part of the charges. On the Bench were Magistrates Lieutenant Pascoe of the Water Police, Captain Ferguson Harbour Master, and Lieutenant Crawford Inspector of the Water Police. Mr. Shillinglaw conducted the Prosecution, and Mr. Read presented for James Nicol Forbes.

Captain Forbes appeared on summons. The questions to be examined were, did he, on the day of the wreck,

December 26, while master of the British ship *Schomberg,* neglect to do his duty, or omit certain acts such as drop the anchor or neglect other acts which he properly should do to preserve his ship from loss according to the relevant statute. The charges were laid under the *Merchant Shipping Act* 17th and 18th Vict., cap. 104, sec. 239. One journalist noted that Boatswain Hodge of the *Schomberg* sat with and had "aligned" himself with the Prosecution: the other officers of the ship seemed keen for the acquittal of their commander.[77]

~

Mr. Melville was the first witness called. A newspaper said Melville was unable to answer any of the questions asked. Mr. Saxby, Third Mate, was called to give evidence, and he answered thoroughly. Saxby stated he would not have dropped the anchor sooner than they did. Mr. Hodge's examination followed: he said on the fateful night the hawse holes (pipes) were still plugged, "I would have pitched the anchor over the bows." The Court asked Hodge about the *Schomberg* missing stays earlier during the passage, which he had previously stated. When pressed, Hodge said he did not wish to swear to a lie and admitted that he did not know for sure of the vessel missing stays earlier in the passage. The Purser's Mate, Mr. Osbaldistone, was sworn but claimed he knew nothing, having been below decks when the ship struck.

Mr. Read, the Defence lawyer, said the question was not about the chains not being bent to the anchors or the anchors not being dropped unless the Prosecution could show that dropping the anchors would have saved the vessel. What

---

[77] "Proceedings at Williamstown Against Capt. Forbes" *Age* 21 Jan, 1856 p.3

caused the wreck was the charts which did not show rocks and reefs along this shore at the Curdies inlet or the presence of a strong northwest current along the shore.

Mr. McIntosh, the licensee of the British Hotel in Queen Street, was called to give evidence. He testified that a meeting of select passengers with Mr. Shillinglaw took place at his establishment on January 22nd. An amount of money was given by those present to Mr. Hodge, it was said, in exchange for his support in the coming court cases. Hodge had earlier admitted meeting Mr. Melville and half a dozen others at the British Hotel. Mr. Hodge was then called but was no longer in Court. Mr. Hodge and Mr. Melville had left.

Captain Forbes' Defence lawyer in Court at Williamstown, Mr. Read, said if the *Schomberg* had not been lost, "*they would never have heard anything of these charges, but it was because the Captain of the vessel had met with a misfortune, that a lot of contemptible curs now came forward to have a bark at the dead lion.*"

When the Williamstown Court forwarded the case to a higher court, Hodge attended. Other witnesses were also bound to appear in the Supreme Court when called. This hearing began in the latter Court on Thursday, February 21. 1856. Robert Molesworth, Esq., Solicitor General for the Colony of Victoria, presided. Mr. Dawson, Mr. Wright, and Mr. Fellows argued for the Defence. The statute involved was the *Merchant Shipping Act* U.K. Was the Captain sober, diligent, and attentive to his duties? Did he do or cause to be done every lawful act, proper and requisite, to preserve the said ship from immediate loss, destruction, or serious damage? Could the Captain have altered course to save the ship, did he keep a safe distance from shore, did he keep a diligent watch, were the anchors ready, could he have dropped an anchor to save the ship, why did he continue to sail in close to shore?

The writer for one newspaper said: "*The whole of the day was occupied in the trial of Captain Forbes, which terminated in his acquittal, under direction of the learned Judge. This result was easily foreseen as the case against the defendant proceeded.*" [78]

Forbes' team claimed that the sandspit, the reefs and rocks, along the shore in this part of the Victorian coast were not noted on any map belonging to the Captain. Nor was there warning of a countercurrent along the shore. A local steamer Captain was a witness and stated all maps and charts of the area were incorrect. On the question of the anchors being ready, the Lloyd's representative, Captain Mathews, said that when he went down to the wreck in the first couple of days, the Captain's log did not show that the anchors had been assembled. By the time the hearing took place in Court, the logbook was with Lloyd's agent's papers, not in Court. Forbes' sea charts had washed away as the sea invaded the ship. Forbes' Officers testified that they would not have cast the anchor at any time before the Captain gave the command. Doing so would not have saved the ship. Mr. Hodge, the Boatswain, was the only crew member in Court to say otherwise. Mr. Hodge claimed Forbes had said as they hit the reef, "no matter, the insurance is correct." When asked if anyone else heard this statement about insurance, Hodge said he thought not. James Connolly said he couldn't give evidence because he spent the whole night below deck. Patrick Brian appeared to know nothing about the case. John Stewart, a crew member in the ship, said he saw the

---

[78] "Criminal Sessions" *Argus* 22 Feb, 1856 p.6

Captain on deck several times on the evening of the disaster. Stewart added that if the crew had cleared the hawse pipes for the anchors, seawater would have soaked the sailors' and the Seconds' bedding and trunks. Captain Mathews of Lloyds said the ship lay about 3/4 of a mile from shore. He would not have let the anchor go. He added captains are not infallible. The shipbuilders had omitted to add bucklers to the hawse pipes, hence the trouble with water below decks.

In the end, the Solicitor General, Mr. Molesworth, found no satisfactory evidence supporting the charges presented to the Court: "the evidence was very unsatisfactory from a nautical point of view." Mr. Dawson, one of the lawyers for the Defence, wished to tell Court that nearly all the passengers from the First Cabin, all of the *Schomberg's* Officers, and roughly 20 merchant ship captains were present in Court to support Captain Forbes if needed. Forbes was not required to testify. The jury was instructed to and did return a verdict of not guilty.

The wild unsworn claims made at the rowdy Passengers Meeting on January 3rd aroused public indignation. Most of the outspoken men from that public forum were no longer present at the hearings; only Mr. Melville, Mr. Carpenter, and Mr. Hodge remained. The Police Court had ordered that they attend. Mr. Hodge and Mr. Osbaldistone said they believed Mr. Shillinglaw might provide them with a position in the mounted or the water police in return for appearing for the prosecution.

Once the charges were examined by the Court, under oath, witnesses like Hodge and Mr. Melville, and Mr. Carpenter, who admitted he gave exaggerated evidence, were seen as unreliable. The Prosecution had not shown that Captain Forbes neglected to do any act which would have preserved his ship from ruin. If the anchor had been cast earlier when the ship failed to obey the helm, they still were likely to strike the reef: lives may have been lost.

Why did Forbes attempt to catch an offshore breeze to give them progress? In his previous voyage to Melbourne in the *Lightning*, Forbes had done precisely this with success. A passenger in this ship, Mr. Fenwick, wrote in his diary when they were near Cape Bridgewater, Forbes was obliged to tack about to find wind. A breeze off the land arrived during the night and sent them on their way. Before long, they passed between Cape Otway and King Island and entered Bass Strait. One more day, and the *Lightning* had passed through the Port Phillip Heads. Forbes, in the *Schomberg*, was doubtless hoping for a similar outcome.

Tea clippers returning from China to Britain through the South China Sea often sailed in close along the coast of Vietnam to take advantage of the evening offshore breezes coming of the warmed land.[79]

~

On the next page is an aerial photograph of Peterborough, the Curdies and the Schomberg Reef. Today the spit is less visible. The largest rock, Bear Rock, stands out, but the ship did not hit that. The remains of the *Schomberg* lie along the long wave break in in the foreground of this image. The wreck is clearly broken in two parts, with the bow of the ship lying closer to shore. The photo was taken in mid-summer hence the relatively calm sea.

---

[79] https://en.wikipedia.org/wiki/Great_Tea Race of 1866

The next image was found on the web a couple of years ago. Navionics Australia has kindly given permission for it to be included in this work. It beautifully illustrates how the very deep water of the ocean quickly turns to very little depth at all. Critics had asked how this sudden change of depth could have been the case.

N.B. this chart is not to be used for navigation.
The indications of depth were added by the author.

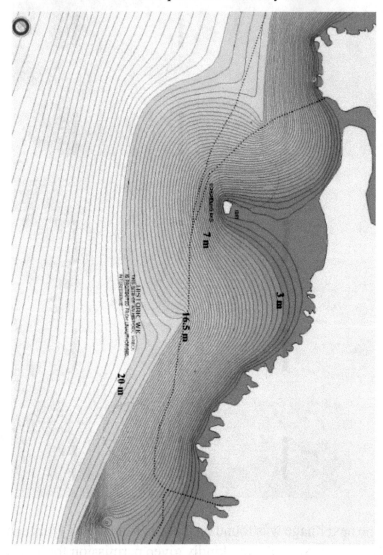

8: Was the Mapping of the Victorian West Coast Incomplete?

In the 1850s merchant shipping companies did not automatically supply their captains with the most up-to-date sea charts to their destinations: mariners had to provide their own nautical maps. In the U.K., it was not until after 1855, and the wreck of yet another large ship close to Britain that parliamentary discussion took place about requiring ships' captains to carry the most up-to-date charts for all voyages. But many regions in the British Isles and the colonies were yet to be accurately surveyed. The western approach to Bass Strait was poorly mapped and remained so after Flinders' circumnavigation for another 70 years, until 1872. There is no way to know how well-equipped Forbes was in this regard. But it was the case that the Admiralty had not adequately studied this section of the coast.

Before 1800, all vessels headed to New South Wales, somewhere between the longitudes of Kangaroo Island and Moonlight Head, sailed south, around the bottom of Van Diemen's Land (after 1856 known as Tasmania). Mariners strongly suspected a body of water ran between the mainland and Van Diemen's Land. George Bass and

Matthew Flinders proved the existence of a strait when they circumnavigated Van Diemen's Land in 1798. In 1800 British Navy Lieutenant James Grant was the first mariner to approach the western entrance to Bass Strait and cross it entirely from west to east. He was delivering to Sydney from London, the brig *Lady Nelson*. She was a small craft of just 61 tons burthen, purpose-built for coastal surveying. The orders Grant received did not require that he carry out detailed mapping, only that he attempt to sail across between the mainland and Van Diemen's Land. He was running low on water and provisions and did not linger, so his map was not much more than a rough sketch.[80]

Two years later, in March 1802, Captain Baudin, of a French expedition exploring parts of southern Australia and Van Diemen's Land, sailed from Western Port Bay in Victoria towards Warrnambool. Nicolas Thomas Baudin, the Expedition Commander, died in Mauritius of tuberculosis during his return to France in 1803. Louis-Henri de Saulses de Freycinet, deputy and then lieutenant of the *Georgraphe*, and Francois Peron, zoologist, completed the printed works that originated in their expedition. The French explorers' party of ships, besides the *Geographe*, included the *Naturaliste* and the *Casuarina*. The next image is an enlargement of a small section of Freycinet's map of "Terre Napoleon," which encompasses the Curdies Inlet and Newfield Bay area.[81]

---

[80] GRANT, Jame*s Chart of the N and W. parts of Bass's Straits* see online at
https://trove.nla.gov.au/work/6721027?keyword=grant%20bass%20strait
[81] FREYCINET, Louis Claude Desaulses de *Carte Generale de la Terre Napoleon (a la Nouvelle Hollande)* / redigee d'apres les travaux executes bord de la corvette le Geographe et de la Goelette le Casuarina par M. L. Freycinet, an 1808

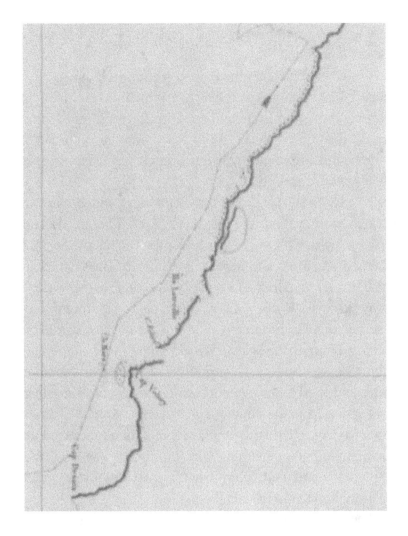

Cap Volney is now Moonlight Head, named earlier by Flinders. Baudin must have come closer to this part of the coast than Flinders. Baudin's map certainly appears to show, west of Moonlight Head, the outlet of the Gellibrand River as an island, the Curdies River as a lagoon, and the rocks and stacks along the shore, which today include the Twelve Apostles, the Bay of Islands, and all the other stacks to the east and west of Peterborough and Port Campbell. The long section of the coast from Moonlight Head west to

Port Fairy has submerged reefs and rocks, the remains of ancient coastlines.

In subsequent years the British Admiralty noted on their maps of southern Australia that they had included the discoveries of the French. The Admiralty did not include the details of Victoria's southwest coast as recorded by Baudin and Freycinet; just the French place names were given where appropriate.

In 1802-1803, Matthew Flinders sailed in the *Investigator* around the coast of Australia, north from Sydney, across the top, over to Timor for repairs, back to Western Australia and across the Bight to Bass Strait and Sydney. He experienced squally weather along what is today known as the Shipwreck Coast. He might have assumed that Grant's map was complete or that Baudin had already charted the coast beyond Cape Northumberland. Like Grant, Flinders was anxious about running out of water and food and wished to avoid the approaching rough winter seas from the Southern Ocean. His vessel was almost unseaworthy. He turned south before Moonlight Head and concentrated on mapping the northern edge of Van Diemen's Land and King Island, and the Strait's many offshore rocks and islands.

The next image is a section of Flinder's map of Victoria's southwest coast.[82] If wholly surveyed, it would have shown what was later known as Curdies River and Newfield Bay.

---

[82] FLINDERS, M. Commander of the Investigator *Chart of Terra Australia Sheet IV South Coast*, created in 1802 first published 1814

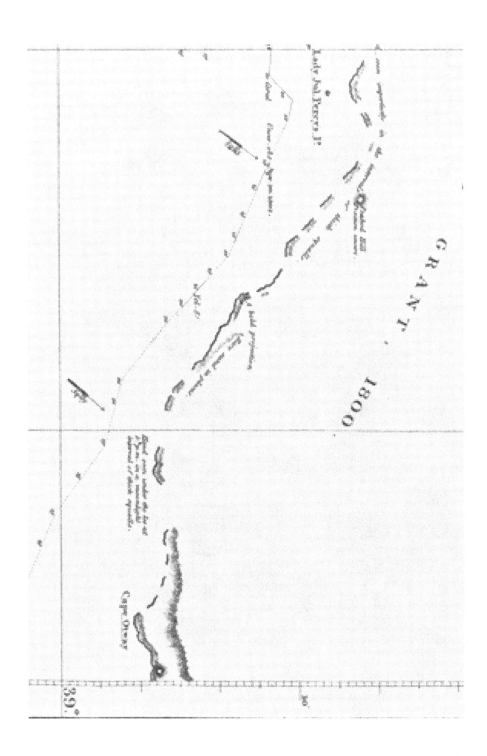

GRANT, 1800

Lady Joh Peters I!?

Cape Osway

35°.

On printed maps that followed Flinders' survey, this part of the coast is shown as a smooth line. [83]

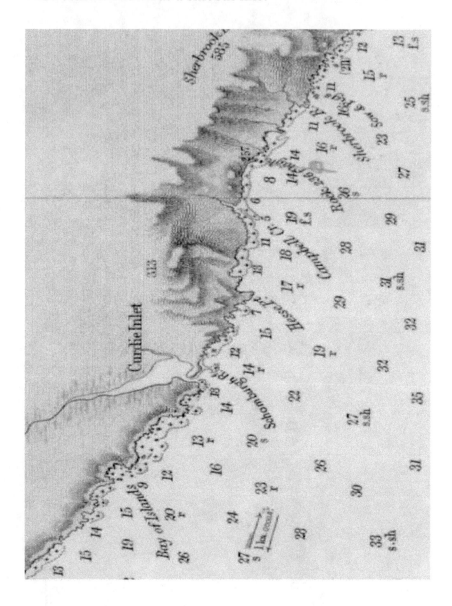

[83] *South Coast of Australia (Colony of Victoria)* STANLEY, H.J. Lieut. G.B. Hydrographic Department, 1872. Courtesy of the National Library of Australia. Johnston Special Collection, 3.

In 1872 the Admiralty's Hydrographic Department did carry out an extensive survey of the southern coast from Cape Otway to the Glenelg River, close to the South Australian border. The previous map resulted from that work.

In Forbes' day, the local coastal steamers, shallower vessels, passed close to shore and knew the dangers of this rocky coastline. With the benefit of daylight, it's a coast that one would not approach. In the dark, Forbes had relied on his charts, the lead line measurement: safe enough one minute, in peril the next.

~

Mr. Allan of Warrnambool wrote to the Editor of the *Age* newspaper and said that Forbes was incorrect when he said the *Schomberg* was pushed to the northwest by a coastal current running from the east and drifted onto the reef. The reverse was true: the ocean ran from west to east.[84] But at times, this seems not to be the whole story of currents, especially those nearer the shore, west of Bass Strait. A book by J. M. MacKenzie, a past resident in the district and school teacher in Timboon, included an account of fishermen who lived in the area. Just beyond the Schomberg Reef, they experienced a deep sea that ran parallel to the coast, to the northwest, then eventually went out to join the general ocean drift to the east.[85] In another of MacKenzie's books, *My Grandmother's Story*, she recorded the loss of the American sailing ship *Eric the Red* close to the Cape Otway lighthouse in 1880. Children of the MacGillivray family, living on the eastern edge of the

---

[84] ALLAN, J. "Wreck of the Schomberg: letter to the Editor" Age 22 Jan 1856 p.3
[85] MACKENZIE, J.M. *Peacock from the sea and Mysteries of the Schomberg*. Peterborough, Vic 1981

Curdies, near the mouth, found the sea had deposited items from this wreck along their beach. [86]

In keeping with this, after the weather and the sea began taking the *Schomberg* apart, Forbes' charts were swept away and were found three weeks later close to Warrnambool, quite a distance west from Newfield Bay and the Curdies.[87] Also, a large iron tank containing a ton of flour from the *Schomberg* was found off Port Fairy, even further west.[88] Some of the wreckage at least was pushed to the northwest, as Forbes had said about the countercurrent they experienced on the night of the disaster.

Perhaps this current had its origin at the entrance to the Strait. The sea is very rough where the ocean meets Bass Strait. Vessels from the west entering the Strait, can face a race, an exceptionally strong stream of water exiting the shallower and narrower, constrained passage of water, meeting the force of the incoming ocean from the west, southwest.

~

In his 1856 letter to the *Age,* also said that, due to their incomplete and incorrect surveys, the British Admiralty must share some of the blame for the hundreds of ships lost over the several decades after the existence of Bass Strait had been established.

.

[86] MACKENZIE, J.M. *My Grandmother's Story.* Privately published.
[87] "Shipping Intelligence" *Age* 21 Jan, 1856 p.2
[88] "Shipping Intelligence" *South Australian Register* 15 Jan, 1856 p.2

9: After the Supreme Court Verdict of February 1856

The Supreme Court found Captain Forbes not guilty on February 21, 1856. He did not hang about in Australia, a sad and dejected man, but returned to Britain in the *Ocean Chief* days later on the 25. He left the ship at St. Ives, Cornwall, on May 12 and made his way home to Liverpool on May 13, bringing with him, as was his habit, some Australian newspapers up to February 25 for local publishers.

News of the loss of the majestic *Schomberg* had already reached England, not by a letter from Captain Forbes or the Black Ball Line's agent in Melbourne. Instead, copies of colonial newspapers which published the wild rumours found their way to London via overland mail. This mail had travelled from Australia to India, by sea to Egypt, overland to the Mediterranean, and then by sea to England. The first newspaper there to relate to readers the wild accusations against Forbes was the *Daily News* of London. James Baines, without delay, wrote a letter of response to the paper and said the Company had only received congratulatory letters from passengers of the *Schomberg*, which the *Vision* had brought home. The Company received no adverse reports at that time. The Company had provisioned the *Lightning* and the *Schomberg* in the same way.

Further, Captain Forbes and Surgeon Hardy had worked together in the successful sailing to Australia of the *Lightning* the previous year. Only the *Schomberg* passage attracted such complaints. The *Daily News* agreed, it was unfair to print the information without giving Forbes a chance to present his case.[89]

Forbes addressed the rumours circulating in Britain and items that appeared in the press by writing to the *Daily News*. He said, in short, the charges brought against himself and the *Schomberg* in Melbourne were unsubstantiated. Even more important to him than his professional character was his moral reputation. Accusers made false claims about the immoral behaviour of Surgeon Hardy and Captain Forbes. Hardy had faced a kirk hearing in his home town in Fifeshire and was found not guilty. Forbes enclosed a letter of support from Reverend Ross, the Wesleyan minister who sailed in the *Schomberg* in the First Cabin. Forbes said he was a man who would not have permitted the gross immoralities with which the two men were publicly charged.[90]

~

Captain Forbes' career in the spotlight was over. He continued to command vessels, but they carried cargo, not passengers. If Baines had continued to place emigrant ships under Forbes, it would have invited rumours and gossip, which would have damaged the brand even more. Reputation was everything. Underwriters might have had some influence over who had responsibility for which

[89] "Schomberg" *Daily News* (London) 5 Apr 1856
[90] "Captain Forbes of the Schomberg" *Daily News* (London) 15 Apr 1856

vessels. The loss of the *Schomberg* had been expensive for the insurers.

~

But Forbes was not without income. Since 1852 he held eight shares in the *Marco Polo*, which he sold to Baines in 1863. According to Michael Stammers, in 1857, Forbes purchased a secondhand ship, the *Hastings,* and sailed her to Australia that year.[91] She was leaky. Lloyds listed this sailing and showed the owner as Baines, so presumably, the *Hastings* sailed under the Black Ball flag. When attempting to sail to Guam in 1857, Forbes had to turn back to Sydney for the dry dock and repairs. While there, he was enlisted in the coroner's inquest in August 1857 into the loss of life that occurred in the shocking wreck of the *Dunbar.* Forbes was considered an expert witness who happened to be in town.[92] From Sydney, the *Hastings* travelled to Guam in September 1857. With the *Hastings* under lease to James Baines & Co., Forbes sailed to Moreton Bay, Queensland, in 1858. The *Hastings* arrived in Wellington, N.Z., in October 1859. A month later, the ship was abandoned and sank off the Cape of Good Hope.

After working for James Baines & Co., Forbes sailed the small Aberdeen clipper *Huguenot* from London to South Australia with cargo in 1860 and 1861. Forbes and the *Huguenot* left Adelaide in August 1861 and headed for Callao, Peru.[93] Another ship he commanded was *General Wyndham*, sailing to Montreal in 1860 and 1866. Forbes was half owner of the *Empress of the Sea*, which burned

[91] STAMMERS op. cit. pp.246-251
[92] "Wreck of the Dunbar: Inquest on the Recovered Bodies" *Empire* (Sydney) 25 Aug 1857 p.4
[93] "British Shipping" *Adelaide Observer* 14 Jan ,1860 p.5 and "Cleared Out" *Adelaide Observer* 24 Aug, 1861 p.5

offshore near Queenscliff, Victoria, in November 1861.[94] Her commander at that time was Captain John T. Bragg. Around 1860 Forbes partnered with John Dixon in a Liverpool sail-making business for a couple of years.[95] The ship *Ajax* was also under the command of Forbes during two return voyages to Montreal, 1862 and 1864.

Lloyd's Register lists other possible sailings with J. Forbes as master: the *Henry* to Quebec in 1853 and 1856, the *Vesta* 1854 to Africa, the *Emigrant* 1860 to Quebec, the *Corredera* in 1861 to Caldera Chile, the *Rondinella* to N. America 1868, the *Kirkwood* in 1870 to Archangel Russia. *Lloyd's Register* referred to Captain Forbes as J. Forbes. But the captain of these last vessels may well have been another with the same name, J. Forbes.[96]

~

In Melbourne, following the wreck of the *Schomberg*, salvage operations began almost at once. The underwriters advertised the auction of the wreck and cargo to take place on the beach at Newfield Bay on Saturday, January 12th, 1856. The purchasers were merchants from Warrnambool, Manifold, and Bostock.[97] The salvagers retrieved some items from the wreck, but the currents at that spot were strong. The wreck and her cargo remained almost complete in Newfield Bay. The paper said in 1856 there had been enthusiasm for retrieving the cargo, but somehow interest in the venture had declined.

The article in the *Geelong Advertiser*, July 1864, said nine years had passed since the first sale for salvage. The sellers estimated the hull of the wrecked ship contained still

---

[94] "Inquest on the Burning of the Empress of the Sea" *Argus* 30 Dec, 1861 p.6
[95] STAMMERS op. cit. p.246-251
[96] *Lloyds Register of Shipping* can be accessed on the web via archive.org
[97] "Wreck of the Schomberg" *Melbourne Herald* 11 Jan, 1856

items worth salvaging: 700 to 800 tons of railway rails, chairs, a significant number of railway axles and wheels, about 140 tons of rolled lead, parts for an iron bridge to cross the Yarra River imported by the Victorian Government at enormous cost, two rail locomotive engines, a large number of lamp posts, water and gas pipes, machinery, quantities of hardware, some thousands of pounds worth of brandy in cases, and much more. The first salvagers had not gathered much from the wreckage apart from loose spars and sails.

The Warrnambool merchants sold the salvage rights again to Mr. Hall, Captain Sealy, and Captain Brookes.[98] These men failed in their first attempt to reach the *Schomberg* site. Two of the new owners, Hall, and Sealy, with rowers, entered the sea from the Curdies. But not long after, a massive breaker hit their boat and threw them into the water. Mr. Hall and Captain Seeley drowned. The four rowers struggled ashore. Mrs. Meek, a sometime inhabitant of the area at the mouth of the Curdies, provided the survivors with hospitality and a horse so that one of them might reach Geelong to obtain help[99]. On September 16, 1864, one of the surviving rowers arrived in Geelong with the sad report. The small boat the group had used to enter the sea was a lifeboat boat of five tons, freshly painted but in an inferior condition.

Over the many decades since the grounding of the *Schomberg*, unknown divers have collected some small items from Newfield Bay. Relics are held for the main part by the Warrnambool Flagstaff Hill Maritime Museum and the Parks Victoria Information Centre in Port Campbell.

---

[98] "Catastrophe at the Wreck of the Schomberg" *Leader* (Melbourne) 17 Sep, 1864 p.8
[99] Article of the same title *The Star* (Ballarat) 17 September 1864 p.4

Today, the *Historic Shipwrecks Act 1976*, with amendments in 2016, prohibits the removal, disturbance, or possession of any items from any shipwreck or its relics in Australian waters.

Pictured here, in 1992, is diver Ron Cashmore, with an anchor from the ship. In the following photo are items from the cargo, riders' spurs. Photo Phillip Doak. [100] Image courtesy of Ron Cashmore.

---

[100] Images from slides taken during a diving expedition, when Ron Cashmore took his friend Phillip Doak, to see the various items worth photographing at different local shipwrecks. Ron Cashmore made these slides available for inclusion in this book.

Below, a photo of miscellaneous debris here at the site of the pieces of wreckage that remain of the *Schomberg*.

The remains of the *Schomberg* were first located by divers from Warrnambool, Stan McPhee and John Laidlaw in August 1973. Peterborough locals had lost this knowledge until Ron Cashmore and others were fishing in Newfield Bay on December 26th 1976. Their fishing net or line snagged on rocks below. Ron dove down to free the net and re-discovered the outline of the *Schomberg* on the sea bed. Years later, in the early 1990s, Ron took friend Phillip Doak to various wrecks he knew along the Shipwreck Coast to make photographic records, with still and movie cameras. After Phillip's death some of his slides were deposited in the State Library of Victoria so his underwater images can be viewed online.

Below, Ron Cashmore is the diver, photographing the iron railway lines which were being carried by the *Schomberg*.

Forbes and the crew who gave evidence at the hearings, described the area where they ran aground as a sandspit. Today any sand which may have covered the submerged solid rock reef has gone. The reef is entirely of rock.

What remains of the sandy spit above the water is less visible than in decades past. In earlier days it was still quite large and one Peterborough family on occasion took a horse and cart onto the sandy spit for picnics.[101] Along this part of the coast of Victoria, the eroding effects of the wind and the sea constantly reshape the bay and the beaches. In 1903, an earthquake occurred offshore near Warrnambool, which gave the area a good shaking. The *Schomberg*'s remains lie in about 30 feet of water, with just the ship's shape discernible in the concreted debris on the seafloor. The currents in the sea are very strong in this location: swimming at this spot is dangerous and not advised.

The following image is of the *Young Australian* which was run ashore in 1877. On the left-hand edge of the image is the inlet of the Curdies. The captain of the *Young Australian* told the courts the vessel had poor sails and rigging and was caught in a storm and destroyed. The image shows the rocky sandspit as quite substantial, with one tall rock which remains visible. Locals know this tall rock as Bear Rock. The whole reef today, not surprisingly, is called

THE WRECKED SHIP YOUNG AUSTRALIAN, CURDIE'S INLET.

---

[101] MOORE, Michael *Peterborough, Please Slow Down.* Publisher's Apprentice, Connor Court Pub., Ballarat Vic. 2014.

the Schomberg Reef. Under the water, beyond this picture, the ancient reef extends far and wide.[102]

~

Mrs. J.M. (Jean MacDonald) MacKenzie wrote a few stories about the ships lost along this coast. One book, the *Mysteries of the Schomberg*,[103] examined reports from New Zealand in the 1860s of large pieces of wreckage found on the western coast of the southern island, which matched the characteristics of the *Schomberg*. Adventurers who found the wreckage also found a ship's figurehead washed up several miles to the south. An American explorer Dr. James Hector, visiting New Zealand in 1871, searched for the wreckage, found it, and sent his report to the New Zealand Institute. At a meeting of the Institute, Dr. Hector displayed a piece of timber from the wreck, measuring 27 feet by 12 feet. Shipbuilders had constructed this piece with several layers, some on the diagonal, joined together by wooden treenails, as had been the *Schomberg*. Scientists sent a fragment of this timber to the shipbuilders Halls of Aberdeen. A reply from Halls said they believed it was consistent with timber from the *Schomberg*. The *Schomberg* was strongly built. But her heavy cargo and the surging tides very quickly caused her, stuck firmly on rock, to break in two. It would seem that a large part of the ship's timber was wrenched away in Newfield Bay and then perhaps was carried to the east, being washed ashore at Tauperikaka Creek, N.Z. The ship's figurehead, which men had talked about for years, was no longer around when Dr.

---

[102] GEORGE, Hugh "Wrecked Ship Young Australian, Curdie's Inlet" Melbourne, Hugh George for Wilson and MacKinnon, proprietors of the *Argus* newspaper, 1877. Courtesy of the State Library of Victoria.
[103] MACKENZIE J.M. *Mysteries of the Schomberg*. Published by the author, Peterborough, Vic. 1970, 1982.

Hector went searching.[104]

It was not the loss of the *Schomberg* that led to the demise of James Baines & Company. The vessel and cargo were insured. After 1851 the Company had relied heavily on loans from banks, secured by mortgaging vessels already in their fleet. By the mid-1850s, gold-seekers had entirely removed the alluvial gold from the banks of Victorian rivers and streams. The work to retrieve gold then involved digging to great depths and building shafts and generally became the business of mining companies. The number of migrants declined. Shipping companies with vessels under sail had not seen this coming.

~

In Britain, there was a banking crisis in 1866. Overend, Gurney & Company, a London bank referred to as the bankers' bank, was declared bankrupt with massive debts. This bankruptcy caused a generalised crisis in the money market and a bank run for others, including Liverpool's Barned's Bank, which Baines used. Administrators declared Barned's bankrupt, unable to meet its liabilities with its assets and income. James Baines & Co. was one of six debtors who together owed Barned's more than one million pounds. Baines had listed ten ships as security for the loans: these and many more were sold in repayment. The total number of vessels forfeited in the liquidation of 1866-67 was 49 of James Baines & Co.'s 61 ships.[105] A well-soaked, second-hand, soft-timber ship was worth less and less with age.

When business first started to decline for Baines, after 1857, five ships that were lost within a year from their fleet

---

[104] MACKENZIE ibid. and "Scientific" *New Zealand Mail* 10 Jul ,1875 p.5
[105] STAMMERS, Michael K. op. cit. p.220-221

were not replaced, and one or two of those were superior ships: *James Baines* was lost to fire in Liverpool, *Oliver Lang* after a collision was judged unseaworthy, *John and Lucy* was wrecked near Brazil, *William Kirk* was destroyed in Torres Strait, and *Indian Queen* declared unseaworthy after collision with an iceberg.

In 1859, Thomas Miller MacKay of the James Baines & Co. wrote a letter to the *Times* explaining why merchant shipping companies were struggling.[106] Companies had purchased too many vessels. The years 1852 to 1857 were profitable until the end of the wars of the 1850s. But shipowners had not taken into account the rising numbers of steam-driven craft. Steamship tonnage was in 1850 104,460: by 1855, it was 288,956 and in 1858, 360,204 tons, on the rise with improving technology and economy, and well able to achieve speed in all weathers. Steamships were now carrying much local and overseas trade. The competition was intense. For sailing ship owners, the situation was depressing, and it would require a long and hard effort for Britain's merchant shipping industry to persevere and remain competitive with other nations. In his letter, T.M. Mackay also urged the government to take time to train future sailors for service to Britain. As well as training for the sea, to provide good education so that tars of the future might be reasonable, happy men as opposed to the rough crews of that day who could not wait to get ashore, to alcohol and prostitutes.

After the crisis of 1866, James Baines and Co. reformed with a new partnership in London, consisting of James Baines, John Taylor & Co., Thomas Miller Mackay and Sons & Co. By this time, the wool brokering industry had

---

[106] MACKAY, T.M. "Shipowners' Grievances" *Times* London 3 Dec, 1859 p.4

established itself in London. When the gold declined, cargo ships and wool clippers gradually replaced the emigrant ships. James Baines & Co. and the Black Ball Line chartered ships to continue their business, including the carrying of thousands of migrants to Moreton Bay, Queensland. Then in 1871, the doors closed forever on the James Baines & Company.

10: What About Forbes? Comparing the Accusations to the Evidence

Did those passengers who made the accusations in the first days of January 1856 hope to stir as much public anger as possible and accuse Forbes of everything they could bring to mind so that the court verdict might be guilty? The passengers could sue James Baines & Co. and Captain Forbes for compensation with such a finding.

What evidence can be found to support their claims in the firsthand accounts, the diaries kept by passengers in the *Schomberg* and earlier emigrant ships under Forbes' command, the *Marco Polo* and the *Lightning*? What can we learn about Forbes from these?

~

First, to examine the characteristics that were required of a good sea captain. Melbourne-born sailor, Captain Alan Villiers, 1903-1982, was an amazing man. Not only was he an adventurer at sea, and later a Master Mariner, but he was also an accomplished writer. He described the role and responsibilities of an ocean-going captain of a sailing vessel in his book, *Square-Rigged Ships: an introduction*.[107] Any captain's primary duties were to protect his ship's well-being, her equipment, cargo, and govern his crew, ensure compliance and quick obedience, and look after the morale of the seamen who at times were out on deck in all weathers and at all hours. For a large vessel carrying a few hundred passengers, one might add the additional concerns of large-scale provisioning and the cooking of food. As the master, he should watch over the health and safety of all aboard, address complaints, and manage acceptable behaviour of the various groups, from the uneducated poor to the more privileged wealthy. When a ship left the home port, a captain was given instructions from the owners, but while abroad, he represented the shipping company and managed the owners' affairs, obtaining cargoes for the return passage and complying with port requirements.

Discipline and order on any vessel were essential. Depending on experience, every crew member on ships had a post to which he went when the captain ordered "all hands." Each man had to "know the ropes," the equipment involved, and take the correct action when ordered. He must know all the standard commands. Everything aboard needed to be shipshape so sailors could work quickly. Every action had to be performed correctly, in daylight or the dark of night.

In some situations, Forbes worked with his men when a lot was being asked of them. During Forbes' second passage out in the *Marco Polo*, when they had been at sea for 52 days, there came 16 days with scarcely a break in violent weather, with gale-force winds, squalls, snow, hail, and

---

[107] VILLIERS, Alan *Square-Rigged Ships: an introduction*. National Maritime Museum, Greenwich, 2009.

high seas. Passenger Mr. Greenhalgh wrote in his diary [108] that after one long night, Forbes sent the weary crew to bed and worked in their place with volunteer passengers. At another time, the high sea dragged the First Mate on the forecastle, over the bows, and into the water. He saved himself by grabbing a rope on the way and hauled himself back on board with great effort. By the 15th day of the challenging weather, the ropes were frozen with ice, and the crew was genuinely exhausted. The conditions were the fiercest on day 67. One of the men refused to leave his bed for his shift at 4 a.m. He was struck by an Officer and placed in irons below deck. To ignore a man's failure to obey a command could escalate and undermine the Captain's and Officers' authority. In perilous conditions, a loss of control might jeopardise the safety of the ship and all aboard her. The following morning, Forbes ordered a round of rum for the crew. On day 72 came a sudden white squall that did considerable damage. The wind ripped away the fore staysail and tore the mainsail and the fore topsail to pieces. There was swearing and a great deal of shouting. To be in such a state was dangerous. The heavy gale continued throughout the night and well into the following afternoon. The weather calmed and in just three more days, they reached Cape Otway and Port Phillip Heads. The pilot took them into port once the government inspector had visited.

~

In contrast, Captain Beazley, commanding the ship *Planter* in 1838, was too lenient with his crew, failed to enforce discipline, and brought upon himself a dangerous

---

[108] GREENHALGH, W.C. "Log of the Ship 'Marco Polo' from Liverpool to Melburn" [sic] Appenxix B In STAMMERS op. cit. pp.471-481

mutiny.[109] There were mutinies aboard other ships resulting in the law courts dealing with the offending seamen in the colonies or the British Isles. There were voyages where the captains and officers surrendered all control to the crew, let them get away with stealing the ship's stores, particularly alcohol, and waited until they had their fun and returned to work. One ship's captain, faced with a mutinous crew, armed several of the First Cabin travellers with pistols and cutlasses to protect the ship and her passengers. Compared to such cases, Captain Forbes, it would seem, was well in control of the behaviour of everyone on board and successfully in command.

~

In the *Schomberg*, did Forbes and Surgeon Hardy behave immorally? According to Angelo Palmer, Fanny was the companion of Surgeon Hardy, not Captain Forbes, as is often stated. We might imagine the ladies were the men's companions at dinner and at the card table. Both Forbes and Hardy were men who needed to be available at any time, attending to their duties. For these two to be sitting up late at night, playing cards would be quite normal. Captain Forbes' young lady was a widow, just 20, Mrs. Vagg, was travelling with her infant baby girl.

Angove's diary said there had been a disagreement between the two ladies, who shared a bunk in the Second Cabin. The space allocated in ships' bunks per adult was 18-24 inches by six feet. Mrs. Vagg wanted the 3 or 4 ft bunk for herself and her small child. In addition, Mrs. Vagg had a dispute with her mess companions: she thought she should have a share of their private treats. The last issue escalated into a noisy disagreement with the others, who sent a letter

---

[109] BELL, James *Private Journal of a Voyage to Australia 1838-39.* Edited by Richard Walsh. Sydney, Allen & Unwin, 2012.

to Forbes, asking him to remove Mrs. Vagg. Then the Captain and Doctor became involved. It would seem the outcome was that these two women received what was seen to be favourable treatment, acting as companions to the gents and eating some or all their meals with the Firsts.

If we take Angove's account, Miss Hart found herself locked out of her cabin, not because she was immoral and supposedly came home at dawn, half-dressed, and deserved to be humiliated, as Mr. Melville said, but because Mrs. Vagg would not share the bunk with her.

On December 9, a Second Cabin passenger was put in irons for calling Forbes' companion a whore. Forbes said of this that the man must have been drunk. Perhaps it was Mr. Stockdale or Mr. Melville whom the Officer placed in irons. This would go a long way towards understanding the furor that broke out once the passengers reached Melbourne.

~

Perhaps it was unwise for Forbes and Hardy to have socialised with the two women. Maybe the accusers greatly exaggerated their time with the Captain and Surgeon. They were men on call. Further, Mrs. Vagg had her baby to look after, so could hardly have been in the Captain's company at all hours of the day and night.

But there were two occasions in Forbes' career, noted in the newspapers, where a woman did take Forbes to court. In 1854 a female steward from the *Lightning* brought a charge against Forbes in Liverpool. The newspaper said the officials in court did not read out the nature of the charge and that Forbes was absent in Aberdeen, advising on the build of the *Schomberg*. The case was set aside. The woman asked for 40 pounds. It seems the case did not go forward to a formal hearing, so one might guess she was paid her money.[110] Maybe she had been promised this exorbitant amount if she accompanied the Lightning to Liverpool as head steward. The second instance occurred in 1857, when Forbes was in Moreton Bay with his ship the *Hastings*, he attended a local social function. Afterward, a servant of his host charged him in the Ipswich Court with "intent to commit rape." When the preliminary case was brought, it was dismissed – a very serious charge based on little evidence. While the hearing was taking place, a large crowd had gathered outside the courthouse.[111]

There were examples of emigrant ships that travelled to the colonies where the captain, crew, and a few male passengers engaged in drunken activities with some females. There are diaries where such behaviour caused the writers to liken their ships to floating brothels. One captain did nothing to control the depraved young men and promiscuous women among the passengers. The diarist described the captain as a coward and noted that the married women going out to the colonies to catch up with their husbands were the worst offenders.

According to passenger John Fenwick's diary, Forbes displayed good manners during his passage out in the *Lightning*. He described Captain Forbes as the most civilized man on board. Fenwick praised the Captain for his calmness and promptitude while the danger lasted when during one night, the ship ran unexpectedly among the reefs of Kerguelen. Over time writers have stated that Fenwick pleaded with the Captain to slow the *Lightning* down. But in his diary, Fenwick said it of someone else: Mr. Teevan "didn't see the difference between scaring someone to death

---

[110] "Liverpool County Court" *Liverpool Mercury* 24 Nov, 1854 p.9
[111] "Local and Domestic"*, North Australian and Ipswich and General Advertiser* (Queensland) 23 Jun, 1857 p.3

and killing them outright." That was all he wrote.

Mr. Melville in the *Schomberg* thought Forbes was insulting when he complained to him about the meat he found inedible. On the other hand, Thomas Angove wrote that Melville "rained down thunder" whenever his mess leader made any mistake. None of the shipboard diaries from the Black Ball Line passengers described Forbes' manner with the passengers as rude or abusive. Yet the staff writer in the *Age*, from hearsay, described Captain Forbes to his readers as a man of "brutal manners."

One feels from the shipboard writings that some of the "gentlemen" on board took themselves too seriously. From the diaries of one or two who travelled in the First Cabin in various ships, the writers wondered who would and who would not be a proper person with whom to socialise. In one of her letters, Rachel Henning, during her first voyage to Australia, the genteel daughter of Reverend Henning, wondered just this and found it difficult to find a suitable companion among the Firsts, preferring not to associate with the commercials.[112] She returned to a sister in England and later sailed back to Australia and stayed, transforming into a robust pioneering Australian woman.

~

Accusers said Forbes was drunk on the *Schomberg*'s fateful night. Alcohol was a problem on all three of his ships, especially among the passengers. But against the claim that Forbes was a heavy drinker, Third Officer Saxby in the Court testified he had never seen the Captain drunk. Many writers have, over the years, said of Forbes that he was inclined to make "wine-tinted promises." This was first noted by Basil Lubbock, writing in 1920, long after Forbes

---

[112] HENNING op. cit.

had died in 1874. Lubbock either believed the colonial rumours or liked to spin a good story. Ever since others have reiterated the same accusations. When Forbes was confined to bed for three days in the *Schomberg*, not one diarist suggested he was suffering from a long hangover. Hopkins was concerned for the Captain and was pleased to see him back on deck.

Travellers wrote diaries during three of Forbes' sailings to Australia in 1853, 1854, and 1855. There was no evidence in the diaries that Forbes drank to excess. Many passengers were drunk: it was a constant problem. In each of the diaries, there was a report of a steward who was caught under the influence of forbidden alcohol. In one ship, the drunken carpenter attacked the cook with an axe. In the *Marco Polo* sailing of 1853, passenger Edwin Bird wrote there were fights in the Third Cabin, the effects of whisky drinking. Forbes called all passengers on deck and lectured about being drunk and what constituted unacceptable behaviour. According to Bird, Forbes said he would rig up a plank and send anyone overboard if caught again the worse for alcohol. [113]

Also in that ship in 1853 was passenger Mr. Greenhalgh. His diary said that the Captain's reaction one night to a steward carrying alcohol was rage, *"he struck the man several times, abusing him shamefully by striking him with a large glass ship lamp, cutting his face in several places, breaking his nose."* [114] On that voyage, at least one passenger drank too much every few days and caused trouble. One man was drunk for days. He was put in irons overnight, and when he would not be quiet and continued to call out, using foul language, a piece of iron, which

---

[113] BIRD, Edwin op. cit.
[114] GREENHALGH, C.W. op. cit.

happened to be rusty, was used to gag him, tied at the back of his head. His lips or mouth bled when abraded by the gag. He was then silent and was set free one hour later. The gag was not an unheard-of punishment. The British Royal Navy used such a gag.

Of the above incident of the drunken steward in 1853, Edwin Bird wrote something different in his diary. The night the steward was caught carrying spirits, he "*was tipsy and saucy with it.* [Forbes] *took a lamp from a passenger's hand and floored him with it. He looked quite a member of Heton College* [sic] *this morning.*"

Mrs. Jane Forbes was a passenger on this 1853 trip, her one voyage travelling with her husband. There had been a ruckus overnight between Irish ladies and other passengers. One Irish woman offered to fight any man on board. Mrs. Forbes suggested the Officers place a notice in a prominent place, saying no ladies were permitted to be on deck after 10 p.m. without their husbands. A firm hand was required.

In 1854, Mr. Fenwick wrote that the cook in the *Lightning* had not given the sailors their tea. When challenged, he threw hot water at an Officer. Captain Forbes, when told, "*sprang off the poop seizing the cook like a terrier, dragged him into the saloon as if he had been a child. The man was put in Irons, hands & feet – he had got a caution I suspect. He has never been sober since we left. Many of the passengers have been giving him drink to get favours.*"[115]

In the *Schomberg*, James Hopkins wrote that their steward fell down the stairs having had too much to drink. When he fell, he was on his way to see a friend in irons. He was seen by some Officers who gave him a hard time. The

---

[115] FENWICK, John *Diary* <u>In</u> CHARLWOOD, op. cit.

next day Forbes sent for this steward. The man lost his position as head steward and was fined forty shillings. The passengers were sorry, for he was well-liked. The stewards would have had access to alcohol meant for the passengers but not the crew. Forbes was not a violent man. Apart from his reaction to the first drunken steward in the *Marco Polo,* there were no other instances in any of his ships where he might be accused of being quick to anger.

Punishment in Royal Navy vessels was far harsher, including whipping with a cat of nine tails, flogging round the fleet, running the gauntlet, and ultimately, hanging from the yardarm. Being put in irons was quite usual as a punishment for crew or passengers who threatened a captain's authority in a Black Ball ship or any other ship of the times. Forbes had at least a couple of men placed in irons during the *Schomberg's* passage. Today we would consider this an outrage but it was an entirely normal form of discipline at sea in that day. After the middle of the nineteenth century, severe punishments like keel-hauling were outlawed, but flogging continued in practice well into the second half of the century.

There were no deaths aboard the *Schomberg* except for those of two premature babies and a steward who fell from the ship. At this time, with legislated improvements for the health of passengers on ships, very few individuals died on board vessels. Tuberculosis was occasionally the cause of someone's death and a burial at sea, but such a person would have been ill when they embarked. The diaries did describe passengers suffering from diarrhoea, stomach cramps, and head colds during the voyage. Interestingly, when James Hopkins had a serious headache one night, his brother placed his feet in hot water and bathed his brow with vinegar. When Boatswain Hodge had stomach cramps and pain in his bowels, surgeon Hardy took a quart of his blood and Hodge felt better. We might wonder how Angove learned of this.

~

Did Forbes say, "Let her go to Hell. Tell me when she's on the beach" when the ship was sliding onto the reef?[116] Mr. Melville reported this to the Passengers Meeting. But when the matter was raised in court, Mr. Melville said, "at least, that's what I think he said." Once he was sworn in front of legal professionals, he could not remember anything. He insisted in the Williamstown Court that his first name was Arthur, not William, that he was a surveyor in London, working from home, but added, for some reason, that his name did not appear above the door. When he joined the *Schomberg* in Liverpool, he said his name was William. He was described as a difficult witness in court.

Writers have credited Forbes with making many startling remarks such as. "Hell or Melbourne in Sixty Days," "Fastest Ship in the World." What spoils yarns like these is that the same remarks were also attributed to others, "Sydney or Hell in Sixty days," and at least one other ship supposedly carried a banner saying, "Fastest Ship in the World." If Forbes had said the latter on a large banner strung from the *Marco Polo* in Liverpool, it would have been reported in the Liverpool press and noted in one of the diaries. And Mr. Fenwick in the *Lightning* didn't write that Forbes said, "Hell or Melbourne in sixty days." These are yarns, not facts.

Similarly, over the years, storytellers have said of Forbes that he once, while in Liverpool, jumped out in front

---

[116] "Hell or Melbourne" Exploits of the Notorious "Bully" Forbes". *Argus* 6 Dec, 1930 p.2

of a passing horse-drawn bus and said, "Don't you know who I am? I'm the man who sailed the *Marco Polo*". Another tale said Forbes, when faced with ribbing from two American sailors in Hong Kong, took off his jacket and beat them both roundly. These are yarns. Did Forbes, as some claimed, padlock his sails to stop his anxious crew members from taking the sails down in rough weather? Joseph Conrad, novelist and Master Mariner himself wrote in his experience he couldn't see how this padlocking could be done: he added that a tale had to be believable.

~

When the *Schomberg* floundered in Newfield Bay, it was claimed by the few that Forbes was disinterested, and it was left entirely to Mr. Keen, the First Mate, or Mr. Millar, a passenger, to arrange for the safety of those on board. The captain of the *Red Jacket*, a clipper belonging to the competing White Star Line, passed the following emotive story to a newspaper on his return to Britain. Various papers carried the piece, including *Lloyds Illustrated News* (London), *Liverpool Mercury,* and the *Aberdeen Journal*. It said Mr. John Millar, passenger, as he left the stricken *Schomberg* with others to search for a suitable landing for the lifeboats, cried out loudly for all to hear, for God to help him and let him save every soul on board. Forbes, he said, you stay with your ship. If I do not return, remember I have a family at home, see them when you return to England. A British society rewarded Mr. Millar for his bravery. But more than one passenger wrote individually to the Melbourne papers, as did First Officer Keen, to say this version of events was trumpery. No doubt, Millar suggested to Forbes that he and Mr. Dixon, also a passenger, could direct the rowers from the crew to find a safe landing place. Later the two men and the crew moved passengers between the *Schomberg* and the rescuing steamer. There were letters to the papers opposing the rewarding of Millar for having done what any man would do. There were similar letters when the Governor of Victoria received an award from the Shipwrecked Mariners' Association of Great Britain to present to Mr. Millar in 1858. His passenger companion in the lifeboat, Mr. Dixon, had written to the Association in England and refused the reward. Did John Millar, actually a talented civil engineer in Ireland, England, Victoria, and then New Zealand, weave a "tangled web" and make a claim to fame that he couldn't retract? The papers referred to him as "Schomberg Millar" for the rest of his life.

~

Was Forbes a braggart? When the *Schomberg* was launched in Aberdeen, during the speeches, Thomas Mackay of James Baines & Co. promised a voyage of 60 days and called Forbes "the fastest man of the age." When Forbes responded, he said little more than, "this time, I intend to go like greased lightning."[117] James Baines & Co. made the most of their successes in newspaper advertisements. Some people could have seen this as boasting; "Marco Polo - fastest ship in the world", "Black Ball Line has carried more passengers to Australia than any other Line," and "Captain Forbes' ability and kindness to passengers are well known."

Basil Lubbock wrote in 1920, decades after Forbes' time, as long as square-rig ships were to be found, "*Forbes was the sailor's hero, and of no man are there so many yarns still current in nautical circles.*"[118] From the writings of the diary-keepers, Forbes seems to be a fearless, hard-driving captain who "carried on." That is, he continued to

---

[117] "Launch of the Australian Clipper-Ship Schomberg: the biggest ever built in Britain". op. cit.
[118] LUBBOCK, Basil op. cit. p.25

carry large amounts of canvas, filled with wind, as they ran before a gale, until it became no longer safe to ascend into the rigging. His aim, and that of mariners like Forbes, was to drive ships forward as hard as was possible, to make a "good passage." In the *Lightning*, the Second Mate, while in the high southern latitudes, was reported to say of the spread of full-blown canvas: "Now this is what I call carrying on" – 427 miles covered in 24 hours.

On the idea of a "good passage," Basil Lubbock said the "Black Ball captains were celebrated for their daring navigation." Captain McDonnell, in charge of the *James Baines,* was nearly aground three times while tacking off the coast of Ireland. At one stage, rocks were "*so close that a stone could have been thrown ashore from her decks. It was a lee shore, and if she had missed stays, she must have been lost.*" But as McDonnell said, when asked why he had taken such risks, the captains were under pressure, required by the competitive shipowners "to make a good passage."

What else was in the diaries that Forbes did say? In the *Lightning,* Fenwick reported in his journal, "*the Captain says we must set every yard of canvas, and if that does not make her go, we must put up our shirts.*" Fenwick was amused to see Captain Forbes on deck, looking up at the sails, every second step, and literally "whistling for a wind."

At the outset of the second voyage of the *Marco Polo,* Captain Forbes, when all passengers had been assembled on deck, asked the cook called Doctor Johnson to go below to check for stowaways before they left the Mersey. When Johnson found one, an Irishman, Forbes said: "*Secure him and keep a watch over the lubber and deposit him on the first iceberg we find in 60° S.*" When the owners of the ship returned via the tug to the Liverpool wharf, the stowaway was taken ashore. At the same departure, Forbes was also reported to have said to the gathering on the deck: "*Last trip I astonished the world...this time I intend to astonish God Almighty*". Yet William Culshaw Greenhalgh and Edwin Bird, diarists, were both on deck at this time, but neither recorded these words coming from Forbes. Both men and a newspaper article did mention Forbes' words about the stowaway.

~

A newspaper printed a rumour, days before the scheduled second departure of the *Marco Polo* for Australia in 1853: someone said that most of the crew had refused to join her. That was untrue: all of her crew were already on board. The year prior, a newspaper, reporting on something someone said, wrote that Forbes had committed manslaughter. But when this was followed through, Forbes was at sea when the death occurred.[119] These are the sort of accusations one could imagine being levelled, jealously, at a tall poppy. Perhaps Mr. Baines' extravagant dejeuners and other instances of publicity-seeking set Forbes up as a "smart alec," a "clever clogs," the target of envy.

When Mr. Edward Hulme, a passenger in the *Sultana*, reached Melbourne in January 1856, he picked up a story which he wrote in his diary. "*The captain had a bet with the captain of the ship Kent, a well-known clipper, and declared if he did not beat the Kent, he would knock her [Schomberg's] bows in. On hearing that the Kent had made the passage before them, the Schomberg was willfully run on shore...the most wicked and shameful incident that ever happened on the shores of Australia*" - a rumour in the making. Edward and his family were running late in Liverpool and missed catching the *Schomberg*, so travelled

---

[119] "Captain Forbes of the Lightning" *Liverpool Mercury* 16 May, 1854

to Melbourne in the White Star Co.'s *Sultana* two weeks later. Once he had settled his family in Melbourne, Mr. Hulme walked to Beechworth to find his brothers-in-law at the diggings. An acquaintance warned him, to avoid being beaten and robbed, not to sleep at night where he lit a fire, but to move further into the bush.

~

The reasons given to explain why Forbes may have deliberately destroyed his vessel, put forward by the accusers of the day, indeed by many ever since, have included: Forbes was losing at cards, he was in a bad mood, he had lost his bet to reach Melbourne in 60 days, he was so in love with one of the ladies and was depressed about soon being separated from her, or he was disgusted with the vessel's slow performance.

In a Melbourne newspaper, in 1939, about 85 years after the wreck, the following story was published to mark Empire Week and Queen Victoria's birthday [abbreviated here]: "*The Schomberg moved like a phantom ship on a moonlit sea. The night was calm ... Bully Forbes ...crack skipper of the Black Ball Line...flung down his cards .... a scowl clouded his wind-bitten face. Seeing him like this it was easy for the passengers to sense the roughneck seaman beneath the correct evening dress ... We're getting rather close to land ... Let her go to blazes, tell me when she's on the beach ... and he went below to try to sleep off his ugly temper*".[120] There were other colourful pieces like this in early 20th-century Australian newspapers.

Forbes was said to be a gambler. Gambling, perhaps at cards, was quite a popular hobby in the mid-nineteenth century as it had been for eons and continues to be. Forbes

---

[120] "Saga of Empire Trade" *Herald* (Melbourne) 22 May 1939 p.14

having a bet with others on travelling time in the *Schomberg* would not have been unusual. But the mention of gambling might have made any Melbourne prim and proper lady disapprove. It was all about making Forbes seem thoroughly objectionable.

When the ship reached Moonlight Head, Forbes would have been disappointed that they were still at sea on day 81, but that was not for want of skill on his part. The winds had not been favourable, and his clipper was laboursome with cargo. She wasn't slow on the days when the wind was with them, although it probably took a gale with powerful wind in her array of sails to speed the heavy ship along.

~

Would Forbes deliberately run her aground? One might say, the glorious ship was built in Aberdeen. Forbes had visited Aberdeen, his hometown, to request her construction as an agent for James Baines and Co.,[121] he had some oversight of progress during her build, and when she was mortally wounded in Newfield Bay, he was not certain that she was fully insured.[122] James Baines was a friend: Forbes was godfather to one of Baines' daughters. Would he have been so insensitive to the damage that would be done to his career that had been 20 years in the making? Someone reported to a journalist from the Hobart *Courier* that as the last passengers were taking the small boat to the steamer *Queen*, Forbes was very disconsolate and shed tears.[123]

~

Critically important to merchants and families in England and to businessmen and citizens of the Australian colonies

---

[121] "Launch of the Australian Clipper "Schomberg" op. cit.
[122] "Loss of the Schomberg" *Adelaide Observer* 5 Jan 1856 p.5 Letter from Captain Lawrence who visited the wreck
[123] "Schomberg" *Launceston Examiner* 5 Jan 1856 p.2

were the difficulties with receiving news and mail across the oceans. Communication between England and the far colonies was unimaginably difficult. Briefly, the sending and receiving of mail between Britain and Australia had been a problem since the earliest days. Several solutions had been sought, but achieving faster and more regular deliveries over such distance still eluded them. Sailing ships had been employed as carriers of the post to the antipodes in the past, but by 1854 the business had been given to the more reliable steamship companies, General Screw Co. and P & O. With the onset of the Crimean War these steamships were needed as troop carriers. The British Post Office turned again to the merchant ships under sail. By this time sailing ships had significantly improved the sailing times thanks to a new sailing plan that took them into the region of the forceful Southern Ocean's westerly winds. At first individual voyage contracts were offered for which shipping companies might compete. As the war dragged on, the Post Office offered longer term contracts. The desired goal was fortnightly mail Liverpool to Melbourne. From there, the mail was distributed to the other Australian colonies. The White Star Line won half of this contract, guaranteeing to deliver in one sailing per month and that this would be achieved within 68 days. James Baines & Co., also hoping to win this lucrative contract, offered to deliver to Australia in 65 days. Arriving in Australia on 16 Oct 1853, the steamship *Great Britain*, reduced to 3 masts and with 20,000 yards of sail, in addition to steam and screw, had travelled from Liverpool to Melbourne in 65 days. [124]

According to the author Tabeart the contracts for both shipping lines stated a requirement of 68 days. These

---

[124] "Great Britain" *Shipping Gazette and Sydney General Trade List* 31 Oct 1853, p.329

agreements were dangerous, unrealistic and put pressure on captains to perform better than other sailing ships of the day. Rarely if ever did a ship's captain manage a passage of 60, 65 or 68 days and certainly not on a regular basis. There were penalties for not meeting the agreed targets. In 1855 the fine for not leaving a British port on the scheduled day was 100 pounds per day. If arrival at the destination was over-time, the penalty for the contracted shipping company was 30 pounds per day. [125] Loss of reputation was something else.

First reports passed to the newspapers in Melbourne gave two reasons for the *Schomberg* catastrophe. Forbes was anxious about the days passing and was unaware of the strong currents as the ocean met the coast close to Bass Strait. Was the pressure of late delivery of the Australian mails sufficient for Forbes to take a risk and push too hard on that last day, Boxing Day in 1855?

~

The charges raised in Williamstown Court came to nothing when evidence was shown to be incorrect or inconsistent. But other ships of that day travelled to Melbourne with very poor food indeed, sometimes food left over from the previous voyage. Most often mentioned in all diaries was the meat, smelly, fatty, boney, salty, but also sour flour, and foul water. Sometimes there simply was insufficient food provided. After reading a dozen diaries from different journeys, one would say the food was good on the whole for the First Cabin, but just good enough to prevent people in the lower decks from falling ill. Hopkins wrote in his entries on four days over the passage that they disliked the meat. He said some passengers seemed to just accept it. He

---

[125] TABEART, Colin *Australia New Zealand UK Mails: rates routes and ship out and home.* Vol. 1 Fareham, England : Colin Tabeart 2011.

said he couldn't come at rice being served with meat. Angove wrote once of the strong-tasting fish and pork.

There were sailing ships where the meat was so rotten it was not good enough even for the pigs and was thrown overboard. The cooking food smelled so poorly in one vessel that the passengers stopped the cook from serving it from the boilers. In another vessel, the water tasted so awful that you couldn't make tea with it. Their bread was sour. They longed for some fresh food.

One vessel on the Australian route that kept its passengers contented was the *Kent* of Money Wigram & Sons of Blackwall, London. In the 1853 sailing to Melbourne, she carried 55 crew, eight to ten midshipmen, and 130 passengers. "She was the pick for speed." Small but fast with just two decks. The ship left London on January 27, 1853, and arrived in Melbourne on April 20. But the *Kent* was not the typical emigrant vessel in the 1850s. A passage in her was expensive, 80 guineas for a cabin, but stewards served champagne twice a week.[126] The writer R.A. Fletcher said of the industry that London shipping companies catered for a better class of persons and cargoes in their "beautiful Blackwall frigates," while Liverpool ships carried any cargo and the great majority of emigrants.[127]

Diarist Frederick Hoare, a passenger in the *Red Jacket* sailing of 1854, was on deck when he thought he could see land. He went to the sailors but wasn't believed. He went to the Chief Mate. When the crew finally worked out where they were, the ship was about two miles from the

---

[126] http://www.historic-shipping.co.uk/monwigram/kent%2052.html accessed 3 Jul 2022

[127] FLETCHER, R.A. *In the Days of the Tall Ships*. London, Brentano's Ltd., 1928 p.212

treacherous King Island shore. This was the site of Australia's greatest sailing catastrophe, with the loss of 400 lives in the *Cataraqui*.[128] The crew of the *Red Jacket* said they were expecting to see Cape Otway, not King Island. Once they were in Port Philip Bay, someone advised Captain Read of this ship that his crew planned to flee ashore. He loaded his guns.[129]

Was Forbes' behaviour reckless? Passenger Alexander Stockdale thought so. At the Passengers Meeting, he claimed Forbes sailed so close to two icebergs they encountered that he believed the keel must have passed over some ice. "*Though not naturally timid, he and others shuddered for their lives, feeling that they were in imminent danger of being knocked to pieces.*" Neither Thomas Angove nor James Hopkins was alarmed as the ship sailed near the icebergs. Both men were interested in this very rare experience.

On another occasion, while passing a small craft, the *Schomberg* went so close that she carried away the vessel's signal halyards, and Forbes laughed it off. Both Thomas Angove and James Hopkins wrote about this. Angove wrote: "*We sighted a ship on the starboard bow at 10 a.m. and by 11 a.m. we were very close by her. She had a dead headwind and was making little or no way and sailing in reefed topsails and mizzen sails all furled. She was carrying only four sails and a part of her jib. It was a delightful sight to look at her while we were passing her. Captain Forbes ordered the helmsman to sail close to her and we did so for*

---

[128] LEMON, Andrew and MORGAN, Marjorie *Poor Souls, They Perished: the Cataraqui, Australia's worst shipwreck.* 5 editions 1986-2014.

[129] HOARE, Frederick *Diary of a Voyage from Liverpool to Melbourne* 1854 filmed as part of the Australian Joint Copying Project, M405 (can be accessed through *Trove*)

the fore stunsail boom took away her colours as clean as a whistle. She was a Yankee ship and no doubt her captain felt indignant at the Schomberg's insolence". Hopkins' version: *"An American vessel crossed our track this morning, so close that one of our sails took away her colours. We shot by her at a railroad speed, the Captains spoke but I could not hear what was said."*

~

In Melbourne Forbes was accused of being disinterested in his vessel, his passengers and cargo: too busy engaged with the ladies below deck to see to the safety of his expensive ship. Probably Forbes had been playing whist down in his cabin, but he would have had one ear open, listening to the noises, and been conscious of the movements of the ship. These would have slowed as the wind weakened. The sails would have flapped and flopped. The racket of the crewmen moving about the deck could be easily have been heard from below, and the screeching and rattling of the blocks would have informed Forbes that the sails were being eased. He came on deck and advised Mr. Saxby, the Officer of the watch, to see the ropes were right for putting the ship about. Although he was not on deck for more than 30 minutes before he ordered 'bout ship, Forbes would have been well aware of how his ship was progressing.

~

Sailing ships required tugs to move them away from and back to wharves and steer them easily through harbours, past anchored ships and shallows. Today sailing vessels carry auxilliary motors to do the work previous carried out by tugs. Captain Alan Villiers said that tacking was hard work in adverse weather conditions: *"You may well have to beat - which means to tack against a head wind which will*

119

not allow the square-rigger to lie up to, or make her course when she must slog along into it zig-zagging, braced up first on one tack then on the other...you might have to wear her...and waste hard-won ground, sometimes a lot." [130] With the lack of wind and the presence of a pushing tide, the *Schomberg,* on her final day, ultimately ran out of room.

Mr. Molesworth of the Victorian Supreme Court said that witnesses had expressed an opinion that Forbes had chosen a risky action by sailing close to the shore, suggesting imprudent behaviour. However, imprudent behaviour was not covered by the law, he said. An old-salt from Sydney wrote a letter to a newspaper editor and said that sea captains were divided on the issue of how close to approach any shore. The *Schomberg*'s position when 'bout ship was ordered was some distance to the east of Newfield Bay and 3 or 4 miles from shore. Forbes had not expected to travel in so close to the beach.

~

Running close to land was a standard sailing manoeuvre. The racing tea clippers, returning from China with their valuable cargo, were striving to be the first home with the tea for the season. Basil Lubbock described Captain Robinson with his vessel the *Fiery Cross* taking the usual route home to Britain, down the China Seas, through the Formosa Channel [Taiwan] to the Paracel Islands then, with the fickle southwest monsoon of June, courting the land and sea breezes down the Cochin China Coast [Vietnam], then crossing to the Borneo Coast and repeating the operation. Skilled captains knew the hour of the night when the offshore breeze from a warm land might spring up.[131]

---

[130] VILLIERS op cit. p.27
[131] LUBBOCK, Basil *China Clippers*. 5th ed. Glasgow, James Brown & Son, 1922 p.223-4.

~

The *Schomberg* was on her maiden voyage. One mariner said that all ships had their traits. When the Court asked Boatswain Hodge, he said he didn't know if the vessel had missed stays earlier in the passage. In fact, Forbes did try to 'bout ship earlier in the sailing when they were briefly off course and without much wind. She did not respond, and he had to wear ship which she did. Perhaps the heavy cargo played a part. Commissioner *Schomberg* in Liverpool gave a report via a Select Committee to the House of Commons in 1854 about the loss of life in emigrant ships and the number of maritime accidents occurring in vessels carrying large quantities of iron cargo, making the ships laboursome.[132]

The two old colonists who spoke to the Melbourne paper thought the *Schomberg* was overloaded.[133] Also, Mr. John Walker wrote to Baines & Co. in a letter carried back to Liverpool mid-voyage by the *Vision*. It said, "I *think it a pity we had such a heavy cargo in the first trip; if we had not, we would have made the passage in fifty days*" and continued "*I formed a very high opinion of Captain Forbes as a most expert seaman, and well qualified in every respect for his important charge...kind and attentive to all classes of passengers.*"

In his last days, Joseph Conrad was working on an essay entitled "Legends," about mariners. James Nicol Forbes was the only person Conrad managed to write about. He thought Forbes was simply a success due to good fortune. Conrad also wrote that Forbes' character was not suited to the demands of a Master Mariner: at the first sign of

---

[132] "Emigrant Ships" *Sydney Morning Herald* 10 Nov 1854 p.3
[133] "Wreck of the Schomberg: all on board saved" *Argus* 29 Dec, 1855 p.4

disaster, he fell apart. In this essay about legendary sailors, he also warned against believing stories that were not credible. Conrad had only heard one side of the tale. Forbes was considered a hero at the start of the passage, in October 1855, then reduced to a poor specimen of a man twelve weeks later by a group of men in Melbourne.

Weather for sailing ships was all important, and made all the difference. But Forbes paid attention to, and worked his ships. Mr. Towson of Liverpool had declared Forbes an expert navigator. When he studied the 1852 log of the *Marco Polo*, he said Forbes had hardly varied from the plan he had provided. Forbes was famous for constantly adjusting his sails to make the most of any wind. Once, the sailors remarked to a diarist that the current shift was very unusual in their work for Forbes: they had not had to alter any sail, but just before the shift ended, the Captain did order a change.[134] They had to hoist the fore and main royals and the degallant staysail.

At the end of November, Angove wrote when in the southern latitudes with the westerly winds, the jib halyards broke during a storm. Forbes and Hodge immediately jumped up and carried out the replacement. The rough weather continued. At midnight, the Captain sent 50 men to furl the main yard. The wind was so fierce that they struggled in the rigging for two hours to achieve this, a task that usually would take a matter of minutes. Then the chain of the fore sheet broke and hit a sailor on the side of the head, sending him over the forecastle. Luckily a returning sea carried the man back on board and across the deck. He suffered bruising and two broken ribs.

~

---

[134] "Captain Forbes's Acquittal" *Melbourne Herald* 25 Feb 1856 p.5

Why is the section of the Victorian coast known as the Shipwreck Coast? Significant numbers of ships were wrecked or disappeared as they reached the southwest coast of Victoria. Only one-third of the known wrecks are estimated to have been located. Some describe Cape Otway's coast and west of Moonlight Head as iron-bound, harsh and rugged. The winter weather on the Shipwreck Coast is regularly stormy, with rough weather from the southwest. Gale-force winds and massive waves sweep in during storms from the Southern Ocean.

~

Australia's worst shipwrecks of the nineteenth-century include the loss of the *Cataraqui* off King Island in 1845 with 400 lives. The convict ship *Neva* in 1835 carrying women and children was also lost off King Island, taking 225 lives. In severe weather, when the *Dunbar* lay outside the Heads of Sydney Harbour in 1857 the captain mistook their position, and the vessel was driven against the cliffs, costing 121 lives. The *SS Admelia* ran onto Carpenter Rocks in South Australia in 1859; 89 died. In 1866, 59 died when the *SS Cawarra* hit rocks and sank near Newcastle in N.S.W. Hundreds of wrecks around Australian shores took the lives of less than 40 people. Many other wrecks involved no loss of life.

Within a short distance of Peterborough, sailing ships lost include the *Loch Ard* with the loss of 54 lives, and the *Newfield,* a 1267 ton sailing ship barque-rigged on her way from Sharpness, Gloucestershire to Brisbane in 1892, carrying a cargo of salt. Nine lives were lost, but 17 men, with help from local people, reached the beach very close to the remains of the *Schomberg*. The weather was mild. The captain of the *Newfield* mistook one lighthouse for another and ran on rocks at night in what is now Newfield

Bay. In 1914 the Italian ship *Antares*, sailing from Marseilles, was wrecked along this coast with total loss of life of her crew. Her remains were eventually found in shallow water east of Warrnambool, along today's Mepunga Coastal Reserve. Another ship, the barque-rigged, four-masted *Falls of Halladale*, hit reefs a very short distance from the *Schomberg* to the west of Peterborough in 1908 without loss of life. The captain and crew, once ashore, travelled to Melbourne by train from the nearby train station at Timboon. Retrieving any cargo from this vessel was problematic due to the weather and dangerous sea. The *Young Australian,* a three-masted schooner, mentioned earlier, was lost on the beach close to the mouth of the Curdies in 1877. Her cargo was sugar and rum. Although the captain blamed the poor quality of the sails and rigging for her loss, causing him to run her ashore in stormy weather to avoid being wrecked at sea, the owners said the opposite, the craft was not in a dire condition. They said the captain had made an unscheduled stop in Sydney to make repairs. The owners suspected the crew had sold some barrels of rum while in Sydney. When the salvagers removed the cargo from the wreck, a substantial number of barrels were missing.[135]

In the nineteenth century, almost 80 ships were known to have been lost between Victoria's western border and Cape Otway, with another 66 ships wrecked around the wild coast of King Island, on the southern side of the western entrance to Bass Strait. An annual report published by Lloyd's of losses and reasons for British shipwrecks, listed as the major causes: extreme weather conditions, navigational errors, unseaworthy craft, faulty compasses,

---

[135] MOORE, Michael op. cit. 65-66.

and incorrect charts.[136]

~

With the discovery of gold, crews began deserting their ships when they arrived in Victorian ports. In May of 1852, of the total 816 crew of the various ships in Port Phillip Bay, 417 had deserted. Replacement crews were impossible to find. The *Georgiana* in 1852 berthed at Point Henry in Geelong with 372 immigrants from the Isle of Skye. Captain Robert Murray commanded her. About 18 of his crew, heavily armed, confronted Murray and stated their intention to mutiny and head for the diggings. The Captain bargained with these men, offering to let them have eight weeks' leave to look for their fortune if they accompanied the ship to Sydney and then returned to Geelong. Murray fired a gun; a man was dead. The Captain was badly beaten and tied to the wheel. Police captured six of the mutineers, and they appeared before the courts.[137]

~

The Right Hon. Edward Cardwell of the British Board of Trade met in January 1853 with James Baines, Captain Alexander Newlands, and Captain James Nicol Forbes to discuss the difficulty for the merchant shipping industry of desertion in Melbourne by ships' crews.[138] Some writers have said that when the *Marco Polo* reached Port Phillip in 1853, Captain James Nicol Forbes, to avoid such desertion, had the unreliable members of the crew detained and charged with insubordination. When the ship was about to depart, Forbes paid the men's fines and hastened them on board. The *Geelong Advertiser* reported, when the *Marco Polo* was anchored in Port Phillip, that eighteen sailors

---

[136] "Wrecks in 1856" *Times* 9 Mar 1857 p.9
[137] "Ship Georgiana" *Geelong Advertiser* 5 Nov 1852 p.2
[138] "Court Circular" *Times* (London) 19 Jan 1853.

were taken to the Melbourne Gaol, for refusing duty.

On this return to England, like many ships of the day, the *Marco Polo* carried 100,000 pounds worth of gold back to Britain, including a giant 340-ounce nugget the Victorian Government purchased and sent home as a gift for Queen Victoria. Officials estimated the amount of gold carried by ship to England, in just four years, 1852-1856, was 12,295,978 ounces, in value 47,571,983 pounds.[139]

Other ship masters faced the problem of mutiny on their return voyage from Melbourne to England or elsewhere once rich quantities of gold were aboard. Just two examples, the *Sovereign of the Seas* in 1854, returning to New York, and the *Stebonheath* in 1856, returning to London, experienced attempted mutinies.

~

After the Victorian Supreme Court hearing against James Nicol Forbes was closed late in February 1856, the public continued to think he had not been found guilty due to some deficiency of the local courts. Many people totally believed the scandalous stories and had little understanding of the law and the workings of courts.[140] The *Argus* published an article which would have fostered the public's anger, accusing Forbes of deliberate negligence, and said: Forbes was charged with endangering the lives of hundreds of people, with loss of a large amount of property, bringing ruin to penniless men, fifteen thousand miles from their home and friends, discouraging emigration, and injuring the commercial interests of the colony. Why was he not charged at least with theft?[141]

Under the relevant law, the prosecutors presented

---

[139] "Gold Produce of Victoria" *South Australia Register* 9 Feb 1857 p.2
[140] For example, "Case of Captain Forbes" *Argus* 25 Feb 1856 p.5
[141] "Case of Captain Forbes" *Argus* 25 Feb 1856 p.5

meagre, inconsistent evidence: the more serious the hearings became the fewer men stepped forward to bear witness. A lawyer, recently arrived from England, wrote to the papers and asked why more evidence was not presented?[142] The reason for this? There was no credible evidence.

---

[142] SAVILL, Richard Clarke "Case of Captain Forbes" *Age* 4 Mar 1856 p.3

11: First Cabin Passengers' Letters to Support Forbes

This chapter contains evidence in direct contrast to the rowdy claims of the public Passengers Meeting in Collins Street on January 3rd. Many passengers who sailed in the *Schomberg* had taken the next steam service to travel to their ultimate destination or to return to their regional and intercolonial homes and businesses. Of the 490 passengers whose names were officially recorded, approximately 55 went on to Adelaide, 20 to Geelong, 30 to Sydney, and 65 to Tasmania. Some others might have travelled on to New Zealand. At least 300 of the passengers remained in Melbourne.

~

In the week after the Meeting of Passengers, concerned gentlemen from the First Cabin sent letters of support to Forbes. Once all the court cases were over, Forbes or a deputy delivered the letters to a Melbourne newspaper and paid for their publication as advertisements on three consecutive days. [143] Fifteen gentlemen had signed eight letters. They were G.C. Hawker, grazier and politician in South Australia; Charles Fenn, solicitor and politician of

---

[143] "Advertisements" *Melbourne Herald* 25 Feb 1856 p. 6

Adelaide; Thomas Millar of Adelaide; Joseph Wilkinson; David Snow; Carl Unmack; D. Leighton; G. Hamilton; James Cowie, MLC for Geelong; Thomas Hendon; J. Gordon; John Walker, politician, miller, and brewer of Hobart; Rev. William Ross on his way to Goulburn; A.R. Motley, Superintendent of the English and Australian Copper Co. of Adelaide; and James Rolleston of St. Kilda. These letters told quite a different story from that which the press and the detractors had generated. Unfortunately, the letters only appeared in full in the *Melbourne Herald*, although they were mentioned in two Tasmanian newspapers where just the letter of Mr. John Walker of Hobart was included. Rev. William Ross also wrote a letter to James Baines & Co. regarding Captain Forbes. He wrote in part:

"GENTLEMEN, - I take the liberty of addressing to you a few lines in reference to the loss of your noble ship the Schomberg, and in reference to her commander.

Of the ship, I have only to say that I am convinced her equal did not float upon the seas. Of the captain that he was fit for the command of such a ship; no man, as far as I could see, could have been more attentive to his duties than Captain Forbes. At all times he was ready at his post, and considering the calms and light baffling winds we had for thirty days of the passage, our remarkable progress was owing to the watchfulness of the captain.

The Schomberg is now gone to pieces, and as is generally the case in such circumstances, carelessness and imprudence are attributed to the commander. The unfortunate accident happened by closing in with the land, the captain hoping to get the wind off the land. The ship went ashore from want of wind at the critical juncture, and not from want of skill on the part of the captain.

Many reports have gone abroad here, one of which is that the captain was drunk. Now, I solemnly assure you, gentlemen, that he was perfectly sober; there was not a shadow even of the appearance of drink about him.

...the captain's conduct cool and firm in trying circumstances, only owing to his seamanlike conduct that no lives were lost...It is too bad to visit a man with such remarks when there was nothing to justify them at the time."

J. Gordon, in his letter to Forbes, included: "*You were always on deck night and day...You were on deck at least half an hour before the ship struck.*"

Three gents, Messrs. Hawker, Fenn and Thomas Millar from South Australia said: "*during the entire voyage we never saw you in the least intoxicated; being constantly in your society...if you had been in the habit of indulging to excess it would not have escaped my attention...within our knowledge that you usually remained on deck during the night. We deeply regret that rumours so entirely without foundation as those which are current in the town, should be set afloat.*"

Eight men signed one long letter:
"*...we regret exceedingly to find that some of our fellow passengers are doing all in their power to ruin your character as a seaman...you were on deck at all hours, whenever your presence was required. Many nights during the voyage you were so anxious that you did not go to bed at all. We have observed you frequently examining all parts of the ship, even from the highest yards on the masts. You showed forbearance in your treatment of passengers who*

had made themselves conspicuous by their drunken brawls. On the unfortunate night, we all think you showed great coolness and presence of mind, in fact, to that alone we attribute the absence of all commotion among the passengers and the extraordinary precision and regularity with which the sailors obeyed your slightest order in those trying moments. We all know you were on deck several times during the evening and that you were walking the deck for nearly half-an-hour before you thought it necessary to give the order for tacking ship...unfortunately the absence of wind and the strength of the current proved too much even for the exertions of the worldwide famed Captain James Nicol Forbes".

The remaining two letters, from Mr. John Walker of Tasmania and James Rolleston of St. Kilda, contained language such as:

"civility, unremitting attention to the duties of your profession, thorough seaman, ranked second to none, generous and obliging commander, the victim of unmerited abuse...Trust you may yet enjoy your hey-day of prosperity, and be enabled to look down upon your calumniators with contempt."

Mr. Walker also wrote in part: *"I regret to say the unfortunate loss of the noble ship Schomberg appeared to be a case of rejoicing to several parties in Melbourne for as soon as the steamer which took all the passengers arrived at the Wharf, at Sandridge, our captain called out to a well-dressed person, who was standing on the wharf, 'The Schomberg is a wreck,' and the wretch clapped his hands and danced for joy, and ran on board the steamer bound for Sydney to tell the news. I saw too much of the same spirit manifested by parties from whom better things might have been expected, which led me to conclude that you had become an object of envy, on account of the successful voyages you had made to and from the colony. It is stated in an ancient work, anger is cruel, and wrath is outrageous, but who can stand before envy?"*

In another part of that newspaper, the Editor of the *Melbourne Herald* wrote of the unqualified support from the gentlemen, as: *"very staggering to anyone whose mind has been prejudiced against Captain Forbes"*.[144]

Why did Forbes pass the letters from the First Cabin gentlemen to the one newspaper, the *Melbourne Herald*? Perhaps he wished to counter their stirring article of January 1, 1856. Possibly he or his agent had intended to pass them to all three Melbourne major papers and found this not to be feasible.

~

A year earlier, when the *Lightning* reached Port Phillip, passengers from both the First and Second Cabin wrote letters of appreciation to the Captain.

Forbes replied: *Ladies and Gentlemen- It affords me sincere pleasure to receive this expression of your satisfaction with the ship Lightning and her accommodations at the termination of her voyage.*

Had we been at all fortunate in winds, I am confident the Lightning would have fully realised both your and my own expectations of her splendid capabilities, and would have made the shortest passage that has ever been made to this port by a sailing ship. I feel assured she will do so, and

---

[144] "Captain Forbes's Acquittal" *Melbourne Herald* 25 Feb 1856 p.5 and in the same edition "Advertisement: The Schomberg: Letters Addressed to Captain Forbes by Cabin Passengers" p.6

I only hope I shall again have the pleasure of meeting you on board of her. For your kind remarks regarding my own conduct, I beg to thank you. Your cordial co-operation lightened my duties, and materially assisted in promoting the pleasure and harmony which I am happy to say existed during the passage. I shall gratefully remember it, and sincerely reciprocate your kind wishes; and hoping you may enjoy health, happiness, and prosperity in your new home.

I remain, your obedient servant
JAMES NICOL FORBES.[145]

---

[145] "Advertisement" two letters from passengers and replies from Forbes. *Argus* 5 Aug 1854 p.1

12: In the End

The accusations against Forbes, raised by a small group of men, two dozen or so of the 490 passengers and 120 crew, stand in marked contrast to the statements contained in the unsolicited letters described in the previous chapter. Diaries written during Forbes' earlier passages in Black Ball ships can hardly be said to reflect a man who was disinterested in his craft or his passengers, or was cruel and uncommonly violent. In their testimonies, the Officers of the *Schomberg*, except for Boatswain Hodge, supported Forbes. After his very first voyage in the *Marco Polo*, with 960 assisted immigrants and a large crew, Forbes was praised for his ability, skills and his kindness to all, although the task must have been immense.

The maps of the western approach to Bass Strait were sketchy and incomplete. The Admiralty had not closely mapped the southern Australian coast from the Backstairs Passage behind Kangaroo Island to Cape Otway. In 1872 a detailed survey was finally carried out. The damage was done by the presence of offshore reefs, by the loss of wind at a perilous time and by unexpected current in the sea which carried the heavy vessel too close to the shore. It's easy to see a better decision in hindsight. Forbes was under pressure. Maybe he was conscious of his employers' promises to the people of Aberdeen. Perhaps Forbes feared James Baines & Co. would lose their part of the lucrative and prestigious postal contract after a poor performance. This would be to the advantage of their most significant competitor, the White Star Line.

Of great importance was the reputation of Forbes' employer, James Baines & Company's Black Ball Line of Australian clippers. The reputation of the Line might suffer in the long term. But in sailing towards an unfamiliar shore at night, Forbes took a risk, one that did not pay off.

Newspapers in England made no more mention of James Nicol Forbes after 1856, until 1874 when he died, and then one or two papers published an obituary. Admittedly, such notices always compliment the deceased. Forbes was described as an outstanding, hard-driving, daring Captain and an excellent navigator who ran fast ships across the globe. It said Forbes was instrumental in the success of Liverpool as the chief British port of the decade for emigration and the exporting of British manufacturing. At the end of the piece, the writer referred to the deceased Captain as "Aberdeen Forbes, as he was familiarly called."[146] Bully was the seafarer's expression.

Captain Forbes was in the limelight just a handful of years in the 1850s. He was the subject of fanciful sailors' yarns for decades after his death. Seamen "spun their yarns" perhaps ashore, while they sat at the fireside in some sailor town inn chatting, outdoing each other with their stories. Wild tales, tall stories over time have become accepted as

---

[146] reprinted as "Aberdeen Forbes" in the *Brisbane Courier* 21 Sep 1874 p.3; "Death of a Well-Known Sea Captain" *Warwick Examiner and Times* 26 Sep 1874, p.1; and "Aberdeen Forbes" *Queenslander* 3 Oct 1874 p.7, via *Trove*

facts. Some writers have continued to label Forbes as infamous, notorious, as a bully in today's terms, more like a rough pirate than a courageous Master Mariner of the deep oceans. Australian families have passed stories down over 150 years, and the occasional reflections on the clipper era in our newspapers have perpetuated the notion that Forbes was an appalling man. Basil Lubbock, who now seems to be the source of at least one or two of the rumours, said, *"the life of this remarkable man has become shrouded in legend and fairy tale, and at this length of time it is difficult to separate the fact from the fiction"*. [147] Lubbock's publications did not list his sources of information.

Forbes did lie about the readiness of the anchors: he wanted not to be dragged through the courts at a time when he must have been suffering from heart-felt regret and self-recrimination. Why did the accusers in Melbourne tell so many lies? They hoped to gain financial recompense, which they would otherwise not have been awarded. Alternatively, they wished to punish Forbes for their losses and spoil his reputation.

Forbes' character was unfairly tarnished in 1856 by a few men who gave no thought to the consequences for the man they falsely accused. It's difficult to understand the motivation of Melville and Millar, Stockdale, and others. But that was then, and this is now. It seems incredible but must be so: the shocking claims made against Forbes, that began in the public forum at the Passengers Meeting, were completely fabricated.

*   *   *   *   *   *

---

[147] LUBBOCK, Basil op. cit. p.23

Acknowledgements and Postscript

Many, many thanks go to Mr. Arthur Meredith-Smith of Melbourne. He, too, has spent many years gathering information about Captain Forbes and the emigrant ships he commanded, especially the *Schomberg*. Generously Arthur read drafts of this work, gave feedback, and provided many hints, and snippets of information.

Thanks to my husband, and friends who read the text and encouraged me to continue.

Thanks to Ron Cashmore and Philip J. Gray for the illustrations included here.

Thanks also to Mr. Robert New of Tale Publishing in Melbourne for his assistance, his enthusiasm and expertise.

~

Being reliant of the text of the historic newspapers, the National Library of Australia's online database *Trove* for Australian historical papers, and Gale's database *News Vault* were essential sources and frequently consulted. The *Melbourne Herald* for the 1850s does not yet appear in *Trove* but was available on microfilm at the State Library of Victoria. Several of the diaries written by travellers to Melbourne were identified and accessed using the *Trove* gateway. The diaries referred to were full of fascinating information. I have resisted spilling all the beans, so interested readers are encouraged to find and read these. Without the National Library of Australia, the State Library of Victoria and the Public Record Office of Victoria, the research would not have been remotely possible.

~

Just a few of the passengers were tracked after they arrived in colonial Victoria.

Mr. Thomas Angove worked as a manager and consultant in the mining industry in the district of Clunes in Victoria. His family moved to Western Australia in the 1880s. Thomas died in Perth in 1889 at the age of 66 years.

John Hopkins was listed as a draper's assistant in Wotton Under Edge Gloucestershire in the *England and Wales Census, 1851* and he continued to work as a draper in Bendigo. Fine words were written about John when he passed away in 1893 at the age of 61.[148]

In 1851 James Hopkins was an apprentice bookseller in England. In 1858 he can be found mentioned in a newspaper advertisement for the return of his horse, to the Albion Hotel, Sebastopol Flat, near Beechworth. After this it becomes difficult to trace his movements. We do know James died on 29th January 1871, in Wotton Under Edge, where he was born. His occupation then was as a partner in a cheese making business.[149]

Angelo Crotch Palmer, worked as a solicitor in Hamilton in Western Victoria, and died there in 1908. Some of his papers, including part of his unpublished diary, and two letters sent home to family are held by the Hamilton Historical Society.

---

[148] "Death of Mr. John Hopkins" *Bendigo Advertiser* 10 Nov 1893, p.3
[149] *England & Wales, National Probate Calendar (Index to Wills and Administrations) 1858-1995* for James Hopkins 1871 via *Ancestry*

Mr. and Mrs. Melville intended to end their voyage to Australia in New South Wales and perhaps did travel on to there.

In adult life, Mr. John Millar practised as an engineer in Ireland, England, Australia, and in New Zealand where he died in 1876. An obituary printed in New Zealand's newspaper *Colonist* 16 Nov 1876, p.3 "Local and General News," gave details of his achievements including his involvement with Victoria's Plenty Tunnel as part of the Yan Yean Waterworks, as Chief Engineer to Geelong's Water Supply and Sewerage Commission, and consulting engineer to various municipal councils in Victoria and lastly in New Zealand.[150]

Alexander Stockdale, after January 3rd, 1856, could not be identified in Australian records so probably returned home to the British Isles.

~

The Public Record Office of Victoria[151] holds a passenger list for the *Schomberg* and thousands of other passenger ships that came to Melbourne after 1839. The folk in the *Schomberg* bound for Tasmania are not included in the PROV list.

See https://libraries.tas.gov.au/how-to/Pages/Names-Index-content.aspx and search for the word *Schomberg* to find the names of passengers from Tasmanian Archives.

If you use the PROV search bar on the home page and enter the words *Schomberg* and your relative's surname you will reach an online copy of the hand-written passenger list. This may show you how your ancestor described himself as a carpenter, weaver, miller, gentleman etc.

---

[150] "Local and General News" *Colonist* 16 Nov 1876 p.3 from *Papers Past* (N.Z.) online database held by the State Library of Victoria.
[151] https://prov.vic.gov.au/

Diaries and Letters

ANGOVE Thomas *Diary*. 1855.

BELL, *Private Journal of James Bell, a Voyage to Australia*. Edited by Richard Walsh. Sydney, 2011. Print on Demand book from Allen & Unwin.

BIRD Edwin *Diary, 1853*.

COOK, William *Diary kept by passenger on board Abel Gower*, Gravesend to Port Phillip 16 July 1852 to 08 November 1852, from Collections held by the National Maritime Museum London, one of the works filmed by the Australian Joint Copying Project, available through *Trove*.

DAVIS, Fanny *Diary of Fanny Davis, 1858* in the *Conway* In CHARLWOOD, Don *Long Farewell*. Thirteen editions 1981-2022, Burgewood Books, Warrandyte, Victoria.

DUTTON, Walter *Diary Liverpool to Melbourne onboard ship Sarah Dixon 1858*, using *Trove, link to Museums Victoria*

EVANS, Charles *Diary of Charles Evans*. Unpublished 1853-1855

FENWICK, John *Diary*. Ship *Lightning*, 1854 In CHARLWOOD, Don *Long Farewell*. Thirteen editions 1981-2022, Burgewood Books, Warrandyte, Victoria.

GRATTON Annie *Diary of Annie Gratton. 1858, the ship Conway.*

GREENHALGH, William Culshaw *Log of the ship "Marco Polo" from Liverpool to Melburn. 1853* <u>In</u> STAMMERS, Michael K. *Passage Makers.* 1978 pp. 471-483.

HENNING Rachel *Letters of Rachel Henning.* Several editions including Penguin Books, Australia, 1988.

HOARE, Frederick *Diary,* Ship *Red Jacket* 1854 (as filmed by the AJCP) : [M405], 1854-1858.

HOPKINS, James *Emigrant's Journal of his Voyage from Liverpool to Australia in the Full-Rigged Ship Schomberg, October-December 1855.* Held by State Library of Victoria.

HULME E. (Edward) *Settler's 35 years' experience in Victoria Australia and how 6 pounds 8s. became 8,000 pounds* 1891 unpublished, held by Royal Historical Society of Victoria and also available online through Gutenberg.

MEREWEATHER, John Davies *Life on Board an Emigrant Ship: being a diary of a voyage to Australia,* 1852.

PALMER Angelo Crotch Pages from a diary for October to December 1855 and copies of two letters sent back to England which describe the events of the wreck, retrieving passengers' luggage from the hold and Palmer's return to Melbourne. Held by the Hamilton Historical Society (Vic).

Index

CPSIA information can be obtained
at www.ICGtesting.com
Printed in the USA
BVHW032335271122
652781BV00020B/1025